THE RIVER OF LIFE

WHERE LIBERAL AND CONSERVATIVE CHRISTIANITY MEET

Lee Harmon

Energion Publications

Gonzalez, FL

2014

Copyright © 2014 by Lee Harmon

Scripture taken from the New King James Version®. Copyright © 1982 by Thomas Nelson, Inc. Used by permission. All rights reserved.

Scripture quotations marked NLT are taken from the Holy Bible, New Living Translation, copyright ©1996, 2004, 2007 by Tyndale House Foundation. Used by permission of Tyndale House Publishers, Inc., Carol Stream, Illinois 60188. All rights reserved.

Cover Illustration: ID 25085890 © Judith Bicking | Dreamstime.com
(Used by permission)

Cover Design: Henry E. Neufeld

ISBN10: 1-63199-091-8
ISBN13: 987-1-63199-091-5
Library of Congress Control Number: 2014950168

Energion Publications
P. O. Box 841
Gonzalez, FL 32560

energion.com
pubs@energion.com

Dedicated to
Leslie Levi,
my life partner,
for her constant support and encouragement,
and for providing me the strength to speak.

TABLE OF CONTENTS

	Introduction	1
1	Heaven and Hell	5
2	The Second Coming	19
3	The Good News	35
4	The Historical Jesus	49
5	Doing Our Part	59
6	But What About Miracles?	67
7	Faith in God	73
8	The River of Life	81

Introduction

I am an agnostic Christian.

For the sake of full disclosure, perhaps I should define what I mean by *agnostic*. I believe in God; I just don't think we know squat about him. I sense that we are linked by something mysterious, that we are more than matter. I am not agnostic in general, I am merely agnostic toward the Christian depiction of God, or any other personal god, feeling that inadequate evidence exists for one caricature to rise above the rest. Arguing about whether it is Shiva or Allah who is *the Truth* is a little like bickering over the color of Cinderella's eyes. Yet I *believe,* because I have both seen and felt God. I have sat in the churches of various denominations and seen strong people reduced to emotional puddles and then lifted into radiance. I have seen kidneys given to complete strangers. I marvel at Mother Teresa's mission of kindness in the name of God, though she herself felt estranged from the God of her church.

I am a Christian in search of God. Christian, because Jesus is my inspiration and Christianity is my heritage.

Life is a mystery. How do we explain our universe, life's origins, and human consciousness? In the Christian Trinity, we have the Son (the mystery of incarnation, or God-in-us); we have the Father (the mystery of our creation and creator); and we have the Spirit (that "something mysterious," the wave of meaning and purpose which links us). All three are astounding, beautiful, awesome. We Christians tend to combine these three mysteries into one, and then personify their union, though we have no evidential reason for doing so. Nevertheless, I am happy uniting all three under the heading of *God* so that a common ground exists for discussion.

I am also a *liberal* Christian, living in a conservative world. Most of my family and friends are conservative Christians. Conservatives consider apostolic tradition of utmost importance, meaning they seek to emulate the first-century church as best they know how. This is a noble goal, but it can lead to stringent intolerance for diluted beliefs. It's the right way or the highway. Liberal Christians, on the other hand, find the creedal requirements which develop from such strictness stifling and contrary to observation and experience. We see God in many people and places, not just in Christian circles. This can lead liberals to a violent condemnation of narrow doctrine. Intolerance is intolerable.

And round and round we go. As a liberal Christian, I have both stooped to verbal aggression and felt the sting of attack. Both sides *care* so dang much that we can't help squabbling, but this hardly puts a good face on Christianity. If the two sides could merely take one step backward, digging back to the Jesus we both adore, perhaps there could be a unity of purpose. Even though there can never be agreement about religious belief, the Kingdom could nevertheless advance. That is my hope in writing this book.

I've written twice before about religious matters: first about the book of Revelation, and then about the Gospel of John. Both books tell a fictional story set in the first century, and both stories are told alongside a verse-by-verse exposition of scripture. They're both agnostic, in the sense that they approach scripture from a historical-critical perspective rather than espousing any particular belief.

This third work is a little more personal. I find that my passion for the Bible, combined with my description of being a liberal, agnostic Christian, confuses people. So, in this short booklet I hope to provide insight into the way many liberal Christians make sense of the Bible and what we actually believe about Jesus. In a review of one of my books, I was labeled an "unapologetic liberal Christian." That's what you'll read here as well: the liberal view. I have nothing else to offer, as I cannot make sense of Jesus any other way. Yet even if you consider liberal Christians like me the apostate enemy, perhaps it would be good to know how your enemy thinks, right?

I confess, liberal Christian thinking *can* seem foreign. Since liberal Christians do not agree with or believe every word of the

The River of Life 3

Bible, how is it that we can draw such inspiration from scripture and from the Historical Jesus? What makes a liberal Christian tick? How can reading the Bible from a historical perspective render a message so foreign to evangelical Christians?

We all struggle to understand God ... even those who wrote about him two to three millennia ago. The Bible is a journal of a nation growing up and learning about God. Liberal Christians do not expect scripture to be everywhere inerrant, or even everywhere very godly. (Do be aware that the word "liberal" in this instance does not refer to one's political stance, but to a pluralistic and critical approach to scripture.) However, I'd be remiss if I didn't confess that a certain amount of left-wing politics arises naturally from studying and appreciating the Jesus of history. I admit this, fully aware that it does little to endear me to fellow Christians, at least to those of my own right-wing upbringing. Yet I remain hopeful that the two groups can someday appreciate one another enough to reach a respectable compromise that honors the Jesus of history.

Out of this hope this booklet was born, which I hope you will find both biblical and respectful, even if you and I read the same scriptures very differently. To emphasize our commonality, I'll be sure to quote scripture liberally (pun intended).

Let's start with a parable.

Imagine a tree which divides into two grafted-in branches. The root and original trunk of the tree is the words of the Bible and the life of a long-ago man who inspires us still today. This trunk reflects the Jesus movement which began 2,000 years ago, though two millennia of bitter theological argument has obscured its original character. We no longer know with any precision what the tree was first like—perhaps it was a fig tree—but we all have our opinions, projecting upon Jesus the image which best fits our own treasured church atmosphere.

One branch grafted onto this trunk became a mighty red maple, built atop Jesus and the Bible, stretching ever upward toward heaven. Let's call this branch the conservatives. The other branch of the tree grew into a willow, drawing strength from the same Jesus

4   *Introduction*

and the same Bible, but bending to reach back down to earth. It is less a religion than a philosophy. Let's call this branch the liberals.

The leaves of this odd tree intermingle, but they look and act very differently. They view each other with suspicion. They all draw life from the Son-light, but seem to be stretching in opposite directions, as if they reach for the Son in different locations. They trust in the strength of their roots, but against such diverse winds that one wonders if they really share the same foundation.

Is there hope for reconciliation? Will the maple leaves ever convince the willow leaves to lift their eyes heavenward? Will the willow leaves ever persuade the maple leaves to reach out to their brothers and sisters down here on earth? Curiously, both sides echo the same frustrated chorus: "Blast it, man, how can you call yourself a *real Christian* if you ignore what Jesus said?"

This book, then, is an attempt to uncover the roots, and in so doing to explain Jesus and the New Testament from a liberal perspective so that perhaps we can at least respectfully appreciate our differences. Perhaps someday we can even join hands in a common purpose, if not common beliefs.

1: Heaven and Hell

It may seem strange that I begin my book at the end. Isn't the afterlife more of a destination than a starting point?

Well, I'm not really starting here. I'm dismissing the topic up front as being of little importance to Jesus. Let's get it out of the way.

What I hope to uncover in these pages is the kernel; the real gist of the gospel; the core message that Jesus taught. I think this core should be the focus of our Christian doctrine. When we put Jesus back in his first-century Judaic setting, the Bible reads very differently, and it's this authentic picture that I hope to convey. The gospel is not about coercing people into heaven or rescuing them from hell. It is not about reward or punishment. It is about the arrival of a different kind of messiah, with an unexpected message.

For hundreds of years before Christ, Jews had dreamed of a rescuing messiah, someone to set the world right again. Someone with the authority and backing of God, who would introduce an era of righteous rule, and who would lift the burden of oppression the Jews had felt off and on for centuries. In this glorious new age, God would come down from heaven and dwell again with mankind. God's Spirit—which had gone missing for hundreds of years—would again permeate the earth.

According to Christians, the anticipated Messiah came in the first century. The gospel is the good news of the Messiah's long-awaited arrival two thousand years ago, and how everything—the whole world—would now be transformed under the rule of God. Heaven and hell are confusing, obscure topics that miss the point, and if we can't set them aside, we'll miss the point too.

Let's start by dismissing hell. You could say the lead-in story to Jesus' messiahship in the New Testament is the fiery warning of

6   *Heaven and Hell*

John the Baptist. Preaching the arrival of Christ (for Christ merely
means Messiah), but perhaps expecting to be rescued by a warrior
patterned after King David, John held back nothing in the apocalyptic warning he delivered to his fellow Jews:

> **And even now the ax is laid to the root of the trees. Therefore every
> tree which does not bear good fruit is cut down and thrown into the fire.
> "I indeed baptize you with water unto repentance, but he who is coming
> after me is mightier than I, whose sandals I am not worthy to carry. He will
> baptize you with the Holy Spirit and fire. His winnowing fan is in his hand,
> and he will thoroughly clean out his threshing floor, and gather his wheat
> into the barn; but he will burn up the chaff with unquenchable fire."[1]**

What was John talking about? What is this unquenchable fire
that he speaks of? Readers today, perhaps unaware of the first-century setting in which these words were spoken, may imagine that
"unquenchable fire" is a reference to hell. Not so. John's wording
makes it clear that he is speaking in the language of Jeremiah,
the prophet who prophesied the first destruction of Jerusalem six
hundred years beforehand. John is saying the very same thing is
about to happen again, using language typical of Old Testament
prophecies against a nation. Jerusalem is about to be destroyed, says
John, with unquenchable fire.

He was right. It happened forty years later in 70 CE. Jerusalem was set to flames. Let's look at another verse often thought to
describe hell, this time from the book of Revelation:

> **And the smoke of their torment ascends forever and ever; and they have
> no rest day or night, who worship the beast and his image, and whoever
> receives the mark of his name.[2]**

I picked this verse because some would say it presents the most
graphic picture of eternal damnation in the most violent book in
the Bible. But that's not what the verse is about. This verse refers
directly to the destruction of Jerusalem, again in 70 CE, because

---

1   Matthew 3:11-12
2   Revelation 14:11

The River of Life 7

the apostate Jerusalem had succumbed to Rome's (the beast's) influence. This may not be clear yet, but I hope it soon will be.

In this verse, the smoke of Jerusalem's destruction ascends forever and ever, but this does not mean the punishment is eternal. On the contrary: these are *precisely* the words used elsewhere in the Bible to describe the burning of Edom,[1] Sodom,[2] and of Babylon later in Revelation, none of which stretched into eternal punishments, and none of which had anything to do with hell. The Bible's writers in all these cases were merely employing a metaphor which was readily understood by their Jewish audience.

We err when we assume that every reference in the Bible to fiery punishment refers to hell. It's simply not so. John the Baptist came preaching that Jerusalem was about to be destroyed by fire. Jesus stood on a mountain weeping over Jerusalem, knowing her fate in the years ahead. Revelation, surely written after many of the events it describes, refers back to the destruction of Jerusalem many times. This great "war to end all wars" in 70 CE, when Jerusalem and the Jewish temple were razed, provides the backdrop for the period in which all four of the Gospels were written and in which Christianity left the forsaken Jerusalem behind, spreading instead to Gentile nations.

How did John the Baptist know Jerusalem must be destroyed? I suspect he read his scriptures (the Old Testament), which he understood to foretell its destruction. Over and over, God threatened to destroy Jerusalem, and in the typological manner in which scriptures are often understood, John found in these prophecies an eschatological promise. Surely, this evil world was reaching a climax, when God would step in, and he would start by punishing Israel. By the time most of the New Testament was written in the latter third of the first century, John had been proven right about Jerusalem's fate. It was hellish indeed.

With this fiery covenantal punishment of Jerusalem as a setting, then, let's look at what the Bible really says about hell. There are four words in the Bible that have routinely been translated to

---

1   Isaiah 34:9
2   Genesis 19:28 and Jude 7

the English word *hell*, reflecting our translators' understanding of verses that may or may not have anything to do with eternal punishment. All four form an unfortunate translation, since these four words are very different. Here they are:

Sheol - This is the Hebrew word used in the Old Testament to refer to the mystery of what happens to you when you die. In Old Testament lore, all souls, good and bad, descend from the grave into a dark, shadowy underworld beneath the earth, where (it would seem from extra-canonical writings) they probably slowly waste away. As the Jews began to believe in an afterlife, two centuries or so before Jesus' time, Sheol began to be seen as a holding place where souls awaited resurrection. It was never a place of punishment at all, nor of eternal existence. It should never have been translated as hell.

Hades - This may be thought of as the Greek version of Sheol. By the time the New Testament was written, Sheol had morphed into Hades, which is much more colorful than its Hebrew counterpart. The Greeks had many legends about this land under the earth, and actually did imagine it to be a place of eternal existence after death. Portions of Hades were pleasant and portions were not so pleasant. The most famous reference to Hades in the Bible is the parable of the rich man and Lazarus (Luke 16:19-31). In this parable, told by Jesus, both descend to Hades after they die, but Lazarus gets stationed in a pleasant place across a chasm from the rich man, who is in torment. They call to one another across the uncrossable chasm.

Did Jesus really present this story as an accurate picture of life after death? Few Bible scholars think so anymore. The story bears an uncanny resemblance to Greek, Jewish and Egyptian stories known by all in Jesus' day. Scholars have discovered many such similar parables. A doctoral dissertation at the University of Amsterdam identified seven versions of the parable circulating in the first century.[1]

---

1   Douglas A. Jacoby, *What's the Truth About Heaven and Hell?*, Harvest House, 2013, p. 38

The River of Life   9

For example, stories of the dead "carried by angels" into "Abraham's bosom" can be found in the Talmud, as can the idea of communicating across the gulf between Paradise and the place of torment. Jesus is not revealing any new secrets about hell, here. Bible scholar Craig Blomberg writes that "Jesus may have simply adopted well-known imagery but then adapted it in a new and surprising way."[1] Jesus is merely drawing on a common legend to make a point about the justice of God in the age of God's rule on earth. The poor and the rich trade places.

Hundreds of years ago, it was common to interpret this parable literally, but this line of thought has largely been abandoned by Bible scholars. Hades is not meant by Jesus to be a literal description of any form of an afterlife.

Tartarus - This Greek word appears but once in the Bible,[2] where it refers to the abode of fallen angels who await their final judgment. This image, too, draws heavily on Hellenistic lore. It certainly has nothing to do with what we think of as hell.

Gehenna - Finally, we reach the word Jesus used to describe punishment of the ungodly. With the exception of one unrelated mention in the book of James (not about eternal punishment), Jesus is the only person in the New Testament who used this word, and only in discussing the fate of the Jews. While it hardly forms a cornerstone of his teachings, Jesus did mention Gehenna a few times during his ministry. Let's look at an example:

> **But I say to you that whoever is angry with his brother without a cause shall be in danger of the judgment. And whoever says to his brother, 'Raca!' shall be in danger of the council. But whoever says, 'You fool!' shall be in danger of hell fire.[3]**

Jesus didn't actually say "hell fire" here … he said *Gehenna*. A person who calls his brother a fool is in danger of *Gehenna* fire. Our

---

1   Craig Blomberg, *The Historical Reliability of the Gospels*, 1987, p. 22-23

2   2 Peter 2:4

3   Matthew 5:22

Heaven and Hell

English translators replaced this with the word "hell," supposing it was a creative metaphor for an unpleasant afterlife. By associating this word with Hades and Tartarus—translating them all into "hell"—Gehenna became even more unpleasant. But Gehenna is actually a proper name referring to the Valley of Hinnom. It's a once-pleasant valley on the south side of Jerusalem, but which drew the disfavor of God because of idolatry practiced there long before Jesus.[1] Gehenna eventually was put to use as a garbage dump that burned perpetually, a sort of fiery symbol for contemptuous destruction. Where once the dead bodies of enemies and criminals were unceremoniously dumped, it became by Jesus' day a garbage pit for Temple refuse, such as scraps from animal sacrifices. There the refuse was consumed by maggots, flames and wild dogs. Gehenna's stigma as an accursed place thus endured. The King James Version of the Bible leaps to the conclusion that Jesus was speaking metaphorically of eternal damnation, and on your next visit to Jerusalem you can even take a guided tour of hell, but scholars continue to argue about just what this image of Gehenna was meant to convey. A closer translation than an eternal sentence might be this Old Testament punishment for disobeying God:

> **Then it shall be that he who is taken with the accursed thing shall be burned with fire, he and all that he has, because he has transgressed the covenant of the Lord, and because he has done a disgraceful thing in Israel.**[2]

This punishment in the book of Joshua amounts to a distasteful death sentence, whereby the perpetrator is killed and the body burned. It therefore *sounds* like Jesus is merely saying the fate of unlikeable men is to be cast into the garbage dump and forgotten after they die. But there is more. It turns out that Gehenna did indeed have a metaphorical meaning by the time of Jesus. The smelly garbage pile with its endlessly burning refuse had become a symbol of fiery postmortem punishment for evil men, as in Greek mythology. But here's the rub: Every time Jesus uses the word Gehenna, he is referring to first-century Jews. Is Jesus, like Jeremiah,

---

1 See 2 Chronicles 33:6 for an example.

2 Joshua 7:15

The River of Life   11

like John the Baptist, like the book of Revelation, referring to the upcoming destruction of Jerusalem when he speaks of God's fiery wrath? It sure seems so. Not one place does Jesus use the word Gehenna when it doesn't read like a reference to the upcoming war. Take for example this verse:

If your hand causes you to sin, cut it off. It is better for you to enter into life maimed, rather than having two hands, to go to [Gehenna], into the fire that shall never be quenched—where 'Their worm does not die, and the fire is not quenched.' [1]

Sounds pretty eternal, doesn't it? Unquenchable fire? The worm dieth not? But Jesus has lifted this image directly from the writings of the prophet Isaiah:

And they shall go forth and look upon the corpses of the men who have transgressed against me. For their worm does not die, and their fire is not quenched. They shall be an abhorrence to all flesh. [2]

Here we see that Isaiah couldn't possibly have been talking about eternal conscious punishment, the way we imagine hell. It is the carcasses of dead men that are burning and being eaten by worms. So what is Isaiah talking about?

This verse culminates the story told in chapters 60-66 of Isaiah, which specifically refers to the destruction of Jerusalem and its temple. Exactly what happened again in 70 CE. Could Jesus be quoting this verse to emphasize that Jerusalem was about to be destroyed again? Let's look at another verse which sounds like hell, but which probably has nothing whatsoever to do with the afterlife:

And do not fear those who kill the body but cannot kill the soul. But rather fear him who is able to destroy both soul and body in [Gehenna]. [3]

It sure sounds like Jesus is talking about God's vengeance in the afterlife, doesn't it? "Destroy body and soul?" But he's probably not. Jesus is again quoting Isaiah:

---

1   Mark 9:43-44
2   Isaiah 66:24
3   Matthew 10:28

12   *Heaven and Hell*

So the Light of Israel will be for a fire, and his Holy One for a flame; it will burn and devour his thorns and his briers in one day. And it will consume the glory of his forest and of his fruitful field, both soul and body; and they will be as when a sick man wastes away.[1]

Again, Jesus is quoting a verse where Isaiah is writing about God's judgment on Israel. Isaiah compares God's judgment to a wildfire burning down people like trees. When Isaiah uses the phrase "body and soul" he is merely employing an idiom meaning "to completely destroy." Likewise, Jesus is merely highlighting Jerusalem's horrible future destruction in idiomatic speech, meant to be recognized as the language of Isaiah. Fear God, says Jesus, who is able to bring Jerusalem to complete ruin.

Was Jesus able to see into the future, or was he a doomsday prophet who felt he could read the signs of the times? I'll let you decide, but either way his prediction was spot on. Josephus, the Jewish historian who wrote about this war, described Jerusalem's ruin like this:

> Now the seditious [Jews warring against Rome] at first gave orders that the dead should be buried out of the public treasury, as not enduring the stench of their dead bodies. But afterwards, when they could not do that, they had them cast down from the walls into the valleys beneath. However, when Titus [the Roman general besieging Jerusalem], in going his rounds along those valleys, saw them full of dead bodies, and the thick putrefaction running about them, he gave a groan; and, spreading out his hands to heaven, called God to witness that this was not his doing; and such was the sad case of the city itself.[2]

Thus, once again, forty years after Jesus gave warning, the Valley of Hinnom became literally filled with dead bodies—this time, the bodies of Jews. Josephus estimates that over one million Jews died in the war. That's probably an exaggeration, but that's not the point. Can you even imagine the stench of hell—oops, I

1   Isaiah 10:17-18
2   *War of the Jews*, Volume 12.3-4

The River of Life   13

mean Gehenna—with a million corpses tossed over the wall of Jerusalem? God's city itself became an extension of this accursed valley, as corpses filled its streets. No wonder Jesus stood weeping over Jerusalem, anticipating its coming demise, before he trekked down the Mount of Olives to deliver his message of destruction to that proud city.

When Gehenna is mixed with the image of eternal fire, the metaphor gets a little confusing. There is a word in our English Bibles that is very misleading. It is this word *eternal.* The Greek word translated as eternal, or everlasting, in our Bible, is most often *aionios,* from the root word *aion.* An aion is an age or period, much like our English word eon. *Aionios* does not mean forever, the way we think of eternal. It is not necessarily endless, but pertaining to an eschatological age; typically, the promised age of God's rule on earth. Some people in Jesus' day may have imagined the Messiah's reign would be endless, but the word is meant to address depth, not length. *Aionois* speaks more of the intensity of joy or sorrow, as being of divine origin, than it does of its duration. Eternal life is abundant life, wonderful life, born-again God-given life. Quality, not quantity. Eternal destruction is horrific, for the God-loathed.

But confusion over how to translate words like *Aionios* should not surprise us. Eschatological writings beg for the use of apocalyptic metaphor. When writing about the end of their current age and the beginning of the next, writers in Bible times easily slipped into a habit of using symbolic and exaggerated phrases. The use of fire as a metaphor for divine judgment, for example, is so common that it could be considered apocalyptic cliché, particularly when accompanied by the word "unquenchable." Revelation tells us the smoke from the burning of Jerusalem ascended "forever," but you should not imagine an everlasting fire. Imagine instead a fire so horrific that the smoke rises beyond the limits of your vision. In a study of the Old Testament, Edward Fudge concluded that it "utilizes some fifty Hebrew words and seventy-five figures of speech to describe the ultimate end of the wicked—and every one sounds ... like total extinction."[1] In other words, not everlasting torment,

---

1   Edward William Fudge, in *Resurrection* 93 (Fall 1990)

14   *Heaven and Hell*

the way we imagine hell. In a study of the New Testament, John Wenham wrote, "I have found 264 references to the fate of the lost. ... It is a terrible catalogue, giving most solemn warning, yet in all but one of the 264 references there is not a word about unending torment and very many of them in their natural sense clearly refer to destruction."[1]

It turns out that there is very little, if anything, in the Bible about eternal punishment for the general populace. Everlasting torment, whether true or not, simply was not a foundational point of Jesus' message. Jesus himself probably said not a word about hell, though he spoke often of Jerusalem's upcoming demise.

The enigmatic book of Revelation, with its bizarre images that refuse to be easily divided between symbolism and literal depiction, may be your best bet if you feel a need to embrace the doctrine of eternal damnation, but in that book, only the ungodly trio of Satan, the Beast, and the False Prophet are clearly said to endure eternal punishment in a lake of fire.

The first evangelists ignored the topic of hell entirely. You won't find anything in the book of Acts about hell. Paul seemed not to believe in hell at all, instead adopting a doctrine of annihilation for the ungodly. According to Paul, righteous folks join God for *aionios* life, while unrighteous folks are put to death.

As a result, the topic of hell evokes passionate arguments from all sides: traditionalists, conditionalists, annihilationists, restorationalists, and universalists. Is hell an eternal punishment? A temporary place of reformation? Merely a separation from God? Is there even a hell at all? Who knows? I don't.

ᥱᨡ ᥱᨡ ᥱᨡ ᥱᨡ ᥱᨡ

So what about heaven? It turns out that Jesus talks even less about heaven. Some Christians today imagine the *Kingdom of Heaven* as a place that exists up above the clouds, but it is not. Only in the gospel of Matthew will you see this phrase used. Out of respect for the name of God this one Bible writer merely sub-

---

1   John Wenham, *Facing Hell: The Story of a Nobody* (Carlisle, Cumbria: Paternoster Press, 1998), 238,241

The River of Life   15

stituted the phrase "Kingdom of Heaven" for "Kingdom of God."
But in every reference in the Bible, the Kingdom of God exists not
up in the sky, but down here on earth. It refers to the age of God's
rule on earth—an age promised by the prophets of old, that was
to be inaugurated by the arrival of the Messiah.

Christians in the first century believed that this Messiah was
Jesus. Indeed, the most pointed difference between Christianity
and other Judaic sects was merely this: Christians claimed the Messiah had come. Christians were *Messianists*. They were perceived as
a messianic sect, venerating a messianic figure. You can see why the
title "Christian" was at first considered derogatory; how laughable
to think that the failed coup Jesus attempted could earn him the
status of the Jewish Messiah!

But that is precisely what Christians were saying. Somehow,
they insisted, in a manner quite unlike what traditional Judaism
thought their Messiah would do, Jesus did set the world on the
right course. The age of God's rule did begin. Jesus, they insisted,
began the transformation of the world from disorder and chaos
into righteousness and justice.

Jesus taught his disciples to pray not that they would go to
heaven, but that the Kingdom of God would come down from
heaven and infiltrate the earth. The Kingdom of Heaven refers to
the Kingdom of God *from* heaven. "Your kingdom come. Your will
be done on earth as it is in heaven," Jesus instructed them to pray.

This leads back to the promise of *aionios* life, and how differently the Bible reads when we recognize it refers not to heaven but
to the era of God's earthly rule. Let me give you an example:

**Now as [Jesus] was going out on the road, one came running, knelt
before him, and asked him, "Good Teacher, what shall I do that I may inherit
[aionios] life?"**[1]

This man isn't asking how to go to heaven when he dies. He
is asking about the new world that God is inaugurating through
the life of Jesus, and how he can be a part of it. Jesus tells him to
sell what he has and give to the poor—this will help bring about

---

1   Mark 10:17

16   *Heaven and Hell*

the messianic age—after which Jesus makes a bold and confusing promise: "and you shall have treasure in heaven."

It's confusing because we have somehow come to believe we must go to heaven to obtain this treasure! As Bible scholar N. T. Wright would say, if my wife tells me she has a cake in the oven for me, it doesn't mean I have to crawl in the oven to eat it. That God has special treasures in a storehouse in heaven for us hardly means they will be sitting idle up there until we die.

No, "eternal life" is not about heaven. "Going to heaven" is not part of the reward. John's Gospel portrays Jesus as deeply frustrated with the Twelve for their inability to grasp this concept. Consider this riddle in John 14, often thought to describe heaven:

> **In my Father's house are many mansions; if it were not so, I would have told you. I go to prepare a place for you. And if I go and prepare a place for you, I will come again and receive you to myself; that where I am, there you may be also. And where I go you know, and the way you know.**[1]

But the disciples *don't* know where Jesus is going, and they *don't* know the way to the mansions of God. They have forgotten the promise that God would come down to earth to live with us here. So they ask for clarification.

> **Thomas said to him, "Lord, we do not know where you are going, and how can we know the way?"**
>
> **Jesus said to him, "I am the way, the truth, and the life. No one comes to the Father except through me. If you had known me, you would have known my Father also; and from now on you know him and have seen him."**[2]

This teaching proves too mysterious, though, so the disciples try again to nail down where the Father dwells. Perhaps that will tell them where Jesus is going.

> **Philip said to him, "Lord, show us the Father, and it is sufficient for us."**

---

1   John 14:2-4
2   John 14:5-7

The River of Life   17

> Jesus said to him, "Have I been with you so long, and yet you have not known me, Philip? He who has seen me has seen the Father; so how can you say, 'Show us the Father'?"[1]

The poor disciples just do not get it. They keep imagining a literal way, a physical dwelling, a corporeal Father welcoming them home. Jesus insists that you "go to" the Father by stepping into the "way" of Christ. The union with the Father then becomes a reality. The "Father's house" is here on earth. When finally Judas admits his confusion, Jesus explains:

> Jesus answered and said to him, "If anyone loves me, he will keep my word; and my Father will love him, and we will come to him and make our home with him."[2]

So we don't go to heaven to live in these mansions; God comes here to us. The disciples fear they will lose their way once Jesus leaves, but Jesus answers that they have already been shown the way. They just need to open their eyes, when they will see that the "way" to the Father's house is "Christ." In the "Father's house," they will not change locale, but rather the Father will dwell within them!

John's Gospel can be mystical and spiritual, but this much we should recognize: our dwelling with God is this-worldly and immediate, not postmortem. There is nothing in this gospel about going to heaven.

Of so little importance is heaven and hell in the preaching of Jesus and the first evangelists that I personally do not think it warrants a place in Christian teaching at all! We Christians should quit worrying about the afterlife and start teaching people about the good news! The Messiah has come! However you imagine the messiahship of Jesus and the role of God, the gospel message is the same: God is finally reforming this world, and we can be a part of it. I do think Jesus believed in an afterlife, but the teachings in the Bible about life after death are obscure and confusing.

---

1   John 14:8-9
2   John 14:23

Heaven and Hell

For now, I'll leave you with Jesus' own definition of eternal life, which has nothing to do with the afterlife:

And this is eternal life, that they may know you, the only true God, and Jesus Christ whom you have sent.[1]

---

1   John 17:3

2: THE SECOND COMING

With heaven and hell relegated to a minor role, what are we supposed to look forward to? One important difference between liberal and conservative theology is the manner in which the two sides view Jesus' second coming. Conservatives can hardly be criticized for being future-minded. They imagine a glorious day in which Jesus will descend back to earth, slaughter two hundred million people, raise the dead to life, and then fly away with all the good guys to an eternal existence beyond the clouds. Perhaps somewhere in this timeline Jesus remains on earth for a 1,000 year reign and perhaps not.

Liberal Christians and critical Bible scholars, however, often have a hard time with this picture. While it's true the majority of the New Testament writers expected Jesus to come back, they also wrote with an intense urgency, placing all the excitement squarely in the first century … not two thousand years later. How can the second coming still be in our future? The following promises are all made by Jesus:

When they persecute you in this city, flee to another. For assuredly, I say to you, you will not have gone through the cities of Israel before the Son of Man comes.[1]

And he said to them, "Assuredly, I say to you that there are some standing here who will not taste death till they see the Kingdom of God present with power."[2]

Assuredly, I say to you, this generation will by no means pass away till all these things take place.[3]

---

1 Matthew 10:23
2 Mark 9:1
3 Mark 13:30

20   *The Second Coming*

Was Jesus wrong about this? We have seen that Jesus, when referring to the torment of Gehenna, was probably talking about the upcoming destruction of Jerusalem—not eternal punishment. That war was only a generation in the future. If you've read my book about Revelation, you now recognize that much of Revelation refers unmistakably to first-century events. This is reinforced by the repeated insistence in Revelation that everything remaining will be happening "soon." If you've read my book about John's Gospel, you know how consistently everything in that gospel (excluding the final chapter, an addendum added by a later redactor) fits a theology of *fulfilled eschatology* ... the recognition that whatever was to happen in the end times, it has already happened. All has been fulfilled in Jesus.

Paul thought differently than the author of John's Gospel. Paul insisted that Jesus wasn't quite done, that he was coming back, and would be doing so immediately. So sure was Paul that Jesus was returning pronto that he even suggested that people not bother to marry![1] Here are a few of Paul's writings emphasizing the imme-diacy of Christ's return. When he writes of "sleeping," he refers to those who have died, and it's clear he expected Jesus' return within his own lifetime.

> **For if we believe that Jesus died and rose again, even so God will bring with him those who sleep in Jesus. For this we say to you by the word of the Lord, that we who are alive and remain until the coming of the Lord will by no means precede those who are asleep.[2]**
>
> **Behold, I tell you a mystery: We shall not all sleep, but we shall all be changed.[3]**
>
> **And do this, knowing the time, that now it is high time to awake out of sleep; for now our salvation is nearer than when we first believed.[4]**

An interesting note about Paul: He lived and wrote just a few years before the war. If there are visionaries to be found in the New

---

1   See 1 Corinthians chapter 7
2   1 Thessalonians 4:14-15
3   1 Corinthians 15:51
4   Romans 13:11

The River of Life   21

Testament, Paul is among them, for he was right about the coming
Armageddon. But was Paul wrong that Jesus would come back to
whisk the Christians safely away? Were the gospels of Matthew,
Mark and Luke equally wrong in insisting that Jesus would be
coming back within a generation? Consider this observation by one
of the most beloved theologians of our time: C. S. Lewis:

> "Say what you like," we shall be told, "the apocalyptic
> beliefs of the first Christians have been proved to be false. It
> is clear from the New Testament that they all expected the
> Second Coming in their own lifetime. And, worse still, they
> had a reason, and one which you will find very embarrassing.
> Their Master had told them so. He shared, and indeed created,
> their delusion. He said in so many words, 'this generation shall
> not pass till all these things be done.' And he was wrong. He
> clearly knew no more about the end of the world than anybody
> else." It is certainly the most embarrassing verse in the Bible.[1]

An entire branch of Christianity, called Full Preterism, refuses
to acknowledge that the Bible is in error. Preterists recognize how
closely the "big apocalypse," from the book of Revelation, matches
the "little apocalypse" in the Gospels, which all scholars agree refers
to the destruction of Jerusalem in 70 CE. They also recognize from
historical writings, primarily those of Jewish historian Josephus,
how closely the events of this war match the description given in
Revelation. Revelation's promise of apocalyptic, covenantal destruction therefore must be referring to the first-century ... not to
some time in our future. Preterists note the intense urgency of Revelation's message, and how its author insisted that he was already
sharing in the tribulation, which was then expected to escalate into
a climactic war. Armageddon.

Thus, according to Full Preterists, the New Jerusalem (as discussed in the final chapters of Revelation) has already arrived. I
realize most Christians picture the New Jerusalem as something
which happens in our future, yet most of the other symbols of

---

1   C. S. Lewis, "The World's Last Night" (1960), in *The Essential C. S. Lewis*,
ed. Lyle W. Dorsett, 1996, p. 385

22   *The Second Coming*

Revelation can be clearly mapped to first-century historical events. If most of Revelation happened 2,000 years ago, why would we imagine that the last couple chapters present an exception? Why do we ignore what Revelation told its first-century audience quite plainly: that Jesus was coming soon? Preterists aren't being difficult, they're merely taking scripture at its word. Revelation's author insists over and over that Christ is coming soon. Not 2,000 or more years later. Four times this is emphasized in the final chapter alone:

> **Behold, I am coming quickly!**[1]
> **[F]or the time is at hand.**[2]
> **And behold, I am coming quickly**[3]
> **He who testifies to these things says, "Surely I am coming quickly."** **Amen. Even so, come, Lord Jesus!**[4]

Here are a few more examples of the urgency of the message, spread throughout Revelation:

> **Behold, he is coming with clouds, and every eye will see him, even they who pierced him.**[5] (Meaning, those who pierced his side on the cross will be alive to see his return.)
>
> **"Behold, I am coming quickly! Hold fast what you have, that no one may take your crown."**[6] (Written to a church which no longer exists, so his coming could hardly be in our future.)
>
> **The second woe is past. Behold, the third woe is coming quickly.**[7] (Context shows the second woe had already happened at the time of this writing.)

We have a choice, then. We can continue to imagine that, somehow, "quickly" means Revelation's distant future, perhaps 2,000 years later. Or we can conclude that John of Patmos, Rev-

---

1   Revelation 22:7
2   Revelation 22:10
3   Revelation 22:12
4   Revelation 22:20
5   Revelation 1:7
6   Revelation 3:11
7   Revelation 11:14

The River of Life 23

elation's author, guessed wrong. Or we can interpret the message spiritually, and recognize that it all happened as planned.

Full Preterists conclude the Second Coming must have already happened. They reason that it occurred "within a generation" when the Temple was destroyed in 70 CE. They argue that the parousia was not a visible event to biological eyes, as Jesus indicates in John's Gospel:

A little while longer and the world will see me no more, but you will see me. Because I live, you will live also.[1]

According to this line of thought, the judgment happened in 70 CE. The resurrection happened in 70 CE. But if everything has already happened, why isn't everything kittens and rainbows down here on earth? Why do people still suffer? What happened to the promise of God wiping away every tear? The answer, for Christians like me, is summed up in the phrase *participatory eschatology.* Big words, I know, but it simply means we Christians recognize our duty to help bring about the dream of Jesus. Eschatology—the study of the end of one age and the beginning of another—happens how and when we make it happen. Jesus held a vision of a better world, and did his part. If we share that vision, we must do our part too.

We need not do this alone. Jesus promised to be with us throughout the age of God's rule.[2] While I do not necessarily align with Preterist teaching, I do recognize from John's Gospel that Jesus guaranteed he would return quickly to take the disciples "to himself" ... not to mansions in the sky, but to a spiritual dwelling with God. How did this happen for the disciples? How can it happen for us today?

In my mind, the nature of Christ's second coming is inextricably intertwined with the nature of his resurrection. Resurrection is key, as every Christian agrees. If there were no resurrection, there would be no Christianity.

---

1   John 14:19

2   Matthew 28:20

24   *The Second Coming*

So what is the nature of Jesus' resurrection? Did he simply disappear from this earth, never to be seen again, as the Gospel of Mark reports?[1] Did he rise bodily alongside many others as part of a general resurrection, and promise to remain "until the end of the age," as many readers understand the Gospel of Matthew? Perhaps Matthew meant to depict the resurrected Jesus (and all the rest of the resurrected saints that day) as spiritual, not physical? Sometime when you're in a contemplative mood, read the final chapter of Matthew. Jesus' resurrection seems presented as physical, since the disciples "hold Jesus by his feet." Yet the final verse of Matthew depicts a spiritual Jesus who will remain with us through the age of God's rule. Try therefore to discern the point where Jesus slides from a physical to a spiritual body. Then try to imagine whatever happened to all the saints who resurrected that day and appeared "to many" in Jerusalem, if indeed Matthew meant to imply a physical resurrection. Did they crawl back in their graves? Who sealed up the tombs again?

Or do we trust Luke's report, where Jesus climbs out of the tomb, presents himself in a physical body,[2] remains on earth 40 days, and then ascends into heaven?

Should we instead dig clear back to our first New Testament writer? Paul saw the resurrected Jesus not in a physical body but as a light from heaven,[3] and considered his Jesus-sighting to be as authentic as any other. When he writes of those who saw the resurrected Jesus, he makes no distinction between how Jesus appeared to him and to others.[4] "Am I not an apostle?" Paul writes indignantly in that same letter to the Corinthians, insisting that he is as qualified to be an apostle as any other person who saw the risen Jesus. "Have I not seen Jesus our Lord?"

---

1   The last twelve verses of the Gospel of Mark, where Jesus appears to Mary and to others, are known to be a later add-on. Mark's Gospel originally ended with the mystery of an empty tomb.

2   Luke 24:39

3   Acts 9:3, 22:6, 26:13

4   1 Corinthians 15:3-8

The River of Life 25

Were *all* of the Jesus sightings visionary experiences, then, like a light from heaven?

I do not pretend to know what happened that miraculous morning of Jesus' resurrection. The differing stories in scripture may be an indication that a precise, creedal understanding is inappropriate. But as a liberal Christian, the resurrection story that resonates most with me is the story told by John's Gospel. Whatever the nature of the risen Jesus, John taught that he could only be seen by believers. The resurrected Jesus could not be seen with physical eyesight; only the disciples who had been taught how could "see" him. In John's story, Jesus ascends to heaven immediately after his resurrection, but he ascends in spirit, not in body. Mary Magdalene happens to spy Jesus in mid-ascent outside the tomb—note the present tense of Jesus' words to Mary that day: "I am ascending to my Father and your Father, and to my God and your God."[1]

However, after visiting God in heaven, Jesus then comes back to earth!

ဢ ဢ ဢ ဢ ဢ

Israel despaired. Long before Jesus' day, the Jews anticipated the Spirit's return to earth and bemoaned its delay. Christianity's insistence upon the arrival of the Spirit, then, was an astounding claim. To acknowledge the Holy Spirit was tantamount to claiming the "rebirth of prophecy," a clear eschatological sign, for when the prophets died, the Holy Spirit departed from Israel and was not to return until the end of days. The return of the Spirit from heaven to earth would mark the beginning of the age of God's rule. When the Messiah came and conquered, God's Spirit would accompany him, and would permeate the earth. Some taught that there would be a resurrection of the dead at this time, as described by the prophet Ezekiel:

---

1   John 20:17

Then you shall know that I am the LORD, when I have opened your graves, O my people, and brought you up from your graves. I will put my Spirit in you, and you shall live.[1]

Ezekiel isn't actually writing about a literal resurrection when he talks of the spirit returning. His vision of the resurrection of dry bones relates to restoring the people of Israel back to their homeland. However, this verse in time began to play a role in eschatological dreams. So when Jesus rose from the dead, what else were his followers to think but that the promised era had begun? Paul insisted that since Jesus rose from the dead, that meant the general resurrection had arrived.[2] If Matthew's rendition is to be believed, lots of other people resurrected then, too, and his eschatological wording is clear: "The graves were opened."[3]

Ezekiel's promise of a life-giving spirit also became an expected gift from God in the messianic age. The new age, ushered in by a conquering messiah, would feature the Spirit's return. Isaiah said the Spirit would identify the Messiah with its arrival:

The Spirit of the Lord shall rest upon [the Messiah], the Spirit of wisdom and understanding, the Spirit of counsel and might, the Spirit of knowledge and of the fear of the Lord.[4]

In that day, God would rule justly, his Spirit would roam freely, and the world would be set right. The prophet Joel calls this the "great and terrible day of the Lord," and relays this message from God:

And it shall come to pass afterward that I will pour out my Spirit on all flesh; ... And also on my menservants and on my maidservants I will pour

---

1   Ezekiel 37:13-14

2   Paul cannot imagine Jesus' resurrection not being the first of the general resurrection, and he argues vehemently to the Corinthians, "If Christ is proclaimed as raised from the dead, how can some of you say there is no resurrection of the dead? If there is no resurrection of the dead, then Christ has not been raised." A few verses later, he repeats, "if the dead are not raised, then Christ has not been raised."

3   Matthew 27:52

4   Isaiah 11:2

The River of Life 27

out my Spirit in those days. And I will show wonders in the heavens and in the earth: Blood and fire and pillars of smoke.[1]

We see this hope not only in Biblical writings but in other Jewish writings as well, such as the Dead Sea Scrolls. In *Jubilees* 1:23, God promises "I shall create for them a holy spirit, and I shall purify them so that they will not turn away from following me from that day and forever." Today, Christians still call this gift the Holy Spirit (the third part of the Trinity) and believe the Spirit's delivery happened forty days after Jesus resurrected, on Pentecost.

Here we find another controversial claim by the early Christians: Not only has the long-awaited Messiah arrived, but he did indeed bring with him the promised Spirit. No wonder a schism soon developed between devout Jews and those blasphemous Christians!

The apostle Paul is particularly excited about the Spirit in his letters. He writes to the Galatians that they are no longer under the law (the prior age) but under the Spirit's direction (the new age). The Spirit produces new fruit in our lives, he said: love, joy, peace, longsuffering, gentleness, goodness, faith, meekness, temperance. In too many verses for me to quote, Paul indicates that we are a new creation, infused with the promised Spirit, and thus the age has begun.

Paul had a phrase that he liked to use: *brotherly love.* One of the distinguishing marks of early Christianity was its propensity for treating one another as "brethren," greatly beloved. This phrase is so common to us today that we may forget what it really means. "Brotherly," in the original Greek, is disturbingly literal. It might be more correctly interpreted, "from the same womb." How are we to understand this? It confused Nicodemus as well: "Can a man enter into the womb and be born again?" To which Jesus retorted: "That which is born of the flesh is flesh, and that which is born of the Spirit is spirit." Born again of the Spirit, we enter into the age of God's rule.

---

1 Joel 2:28-30

The word translated into "love" here is the Greek word *phil-ia*—meaning a fondness, a close companionship. Thus when the author of Hebrews asks us to "let brotherly love continue," he is saying "let there be a deep and enduring fondness between all who have followed Christ into the new age." Maybe it's time for liberals and conservatives to quit quarreling?

The Holy Spirit's entrance is one more sign, one more way in which New Testament writers indicated the Kingdom of Heaven had arrived on earth. But what, exactly, is this Holy Spirit?

In the Bible, the Spirit is associated with creation. In Genesis 1:2, the wind/spirit/breath-of-God blows across the deep. Thus the wind provides an excellent picture of the Spirit, roaming the earth. Breath is merely wind inside us. To be "born of the Spirit" means to be created anew, embracing the meaning of life intended by God. It is God breathing new life into a person. In both Hebrew and Greek, there is only one word for both "wind" and "spirit." The tendency of the churches of today to conceptualize and personify this spirit costs it much of the meaning. It is wind all around and inside us, cosmic breath, the invisible, spectral life-force.

Try to picture the moment Jesus rose from his baptism in the Jordan waters and felt the Spirit descend upon him. Have you had such moments? For many, it's a once-in-a-lifetime experience, impossible to forget. The moment arrives in transcendental form, and we feel bathed in a foreign substance.

In such moments, it's common to be overwhelmed by an inde-scribable feeling of joy, peace, and love. Many have written about their own brush with the divine, though not always in Christian terms like "born again" or "washed by the Spirit." Here are a few quotes from others, taken from Marcus J. Borg's wonderful book, *The God We Never Knew*:

"Immediately I found the world bathed in a wonderful radiance with waves of beauty and joy swelling on every side, and no person or thing in the world seemed to me trivial or unpleasing." –Hindu poet Rabin-dranath Tagore.

The River of Life   29

"I praised God with my whole heart ... Everything looked new to me, the people, the fields, the cattle, the trees." –English evangelist Billy Bray.

"For a few seconds only, I suppose, the whole compartment was filled with light ... All men were shining and glorious beings ... In a few moments the glory departed—all but one curious, lingering feeling. I loved everybody in that compartment. It sounds silly now, and indeed I blush to write it, but at that moment, I think I would have died for any one of the people in that compartment." –British theologian Leslie Weatherhead, as he rode a train from London.

It's difficult to sustain this "heaven on earth" feeling. For most of us, such moments are rare and precious, and though they have a profound effect, the feeling of love and connectedness to everyone around us dissipates within hours or days. Some of us may need a trigger to invoke heaven: a particularly moving church experience, an enlightening session with a gifted counselor, or a near-death experience. Others have discovered ways, perhaps through meditation or music, to invite the Spirit. But wouldn't it be wonderful to *live in the Spirit* like Jesus?

In John's Gospel, the Spirit arrives from heaven on the day of Jesus' baptism. It settles on him and remains, precisely as predicted by the prophet Isaiah.[1] This spirit guides Jesus through his ministry, until he finally relinquishes it as he dies on the cross.[2] Three days later, an apparently incorporeal messenger appears in the midst of

---

1   John 1:32

2   John 19:30. The traditional interpretation of this verse, "*his* spirit," is not necessarily what John meant. The Greek literally reads, "He handed over *a* spirit." While "he gave up his spirit" is now considered a sort of euphemism for death—the King James Version prefers the quaint phrase "gave up the ghost"—at the time of writing, this expression was used nowhere else in scripture or even secular Greek to refer to death. We need to recognize this phrase in context for what John truly meant, and the uniqueness of this particular death: not merely that Jesus died, but that something escaped from his body as he died. John's emphasis here is almost as if the spirit were visible, as if he spied it escaping, in the same manner that he watched its arrival as a dove.

The Second Coming

a locked room, bearing the form of Jesus, and breathes the Spirit on his disciples. Thus in John's version, the Spirit is granted to the rest of us on the day of Jesus' resurrection, not forty days later as the book of Acts reports, but let us forgive this contradiction and read the story:

That Sunday evening the disciples were meeting behind locked doors because they were afraid of the Jewish leaders. Suddenly, Jesus was standing there among them! "Peace be with you," he said. As he spoke, he showed them the wounds in his hands and his side. They were filled with joy when they saw the Lord! Again he said, "Peace be with you. As the Father has sent me, so I am sending you." Then he breathed on them and said, "Receive the Holy Spirit."[1]

John often calls this spirit the *Paraclete,* a word used nowhere else in scripture. Consequently, we don't really know what the word means. Scholars have proposed different interpretations, from "Helper" to "Comforter" to "Counselor" to "Advocate." The most striking quality of the Paraclete, however, is its identification with Jesus:

And I will pray the Father, and he will give you another [Paraclete], that he may abide with you forever— the Spirit of truth, whom the world cannot receive, because it neither sees him nor knows him; but you know him, for he dwells with you and will be in you. I will not leave you orphans; I will come to you.[2]

Note the phrase "another Paraclete," indicating that the Holy Spirit will be the second of two. This second Paraclete cannot be seen by non-believers, because it dwells *within* believers. Who, then, is the first Paraclete? The answer is Jesus. The Holy Spirit is Jesus, in another form. In these verses, Jesus, still speaking of the Paraclete, promises "I will come to you," and when he comes it will be in the form of the Spirit. Indeed, the passage in John continues:

---

1   John 20:19-22 (NLT)

2   John 14:16-18

The River of Life   31

A little while longer and the world will see me no more, but you will see me. Because I live, you will live also. At that day you will know that I am in my Father, and you in me, and I in you. [1]

Just as the Spirit cannot be seen by unbelievers, so Jesus, when he returns, cannot be seen by unbelievers, for the same reason: he will be "in" his followers. Jesus will not be coming back on the clouds, or in any visible form. He will be coming back in a form unseen by the world. That's John's story, and he's sticking to it.

The Paraclete *is Jesus*. According to this gospel, both Jesus and the Paraclete serve as judge. Both Jesus and the Paraclete come from the Father, both are "sent," both are Truth, neither can be received by the world. Neither can be *seen* by the world, once Jesus resurrects. Scholars have found nearly two dozen such comparisons. For three chapters, from 14 to 16, John pounds us with parallels until it sinks in: *The Holy Spirit is Jesus, back from the dead.* Jesus has become so saturated with the Spirit, so in tune to the guidance of this indwelling power, that the two cannot be conceived apart from one other. It has become his mind and nature; Jesus has become "God" in the flesh, a being worthy of worship. The Trinity is complete, and now Jesus promises that when he leaves, he will bequeath this life-giving Spirit to his disciples.

As Paul writes to the Corinthians, "The last Adam [Christ] became a life-giving Spirit." [2]

Confused? Then I'm not properly conveying the concept of Jesus' second coming according to John's Gospel. In this Gospel, Jesus' Second Coming *has already happened.* It happened three days after Jesus died. Jesus rose from the dead in the form of the Paraclete, met with the Twelve in this spiritual form, and breathed the Spirit on them. This spiritual Jesus did not then fade away, as we would expect, but remains forever, as Matthew promises at the end of his gospel: "Lo, I am with you always, even unto the end of the age." Chapter 21 of John's Gospel was a later add-on, not a part of the original Gospel, so its contradictory teachings should not be

---

1   John 14:19-20
2   1 Corinthians 15:45

merged with the original ending to John. In the authentic message of the Fourth Gospel, Jesus is not coming back a third time, for he is already here to stay.

Thus John's Gospel with its *realized eschatology* is very different from the other three Gospels, and even very different from its own "appendix," the final add-on chapter. Yet I am thankful for this Gospel and its minority opinion, because it swings open the doors of Christianity *as a religion*—not just as a humanitarian philosophy— in a way that I can relate to and stand behind. It presents a paradigm of the resurrection and second coming that I can make sense of, so that I can stand hand-in-hand with my Christian brethren of more traditional faith, expanding the circle of the Kingdom. And it jibes with the message of other New Testament books, which promise Jesus will establish his Kingdom immediately.

Now, I won't criticize you if you believe scripture everywhere agrees on a bodily resurrection and promises a second advent still in our future. I'll only be critical if you pretend there is no other legitimate way to read scripture, and demand a creedal statement aligning with your belief. Such a requirement divides rather than unifies Christians, which only hampers the work of the Spirit.

The Spirit remains with us even today. The *aion* of God's rule began in Jesus' day, when the Spirit arrived from heaven, and continues through today. Do you struggle to feel its presence? If you have trouble connecting with the Spirit, try prayer. Yes, I'm serious, whether you are liberal or conservative. When I slipped from the rank of *believing Christian* into *agnostic Christian,* I confess that I forgot how to pray. I simply could not visualize anyone on the receiving end of my prayer, and felt silly trying. Nor could I bring myself to utter the skeptic's prayer: *God, if you exist, save me from hell, if there is a hell.* Many of you may identify with the class of *Spiritual But Not Religious* (SBNR), yet you need not jettison the connection with the Divine that prayer affords.

I find that many liberal Christian authors avoid the topic of prayer, not knowing quite how to handle it or explain it, so let me tell you what works for me. I pray not to the creator/Father, nor to God's incarnational version, the human/Son, but to the third part

The River of Life 33

of the Trinity … that illusive, mysterious Spirit. In the Bible, the Spirit is the carrier of our prayers to God, interceding for us even when we know not how to pray.[1] I find it easiest if I do not try to personify the Spirit. With this focus, I feel silly praying selfish petitions—a universal Spirit somehow transcends my selfish ambitions—so my prayer naturally steers toward renewing my purpose to contribute to the Kingdom of God. The words of the Lord's Prayer are a perfect utterance, so we'll talk more about this simple prayer shortly.

I close my eyes in shallow meditation until I feel the Spirit breathing in and around me, like Wind. I breathe God in and out, for breath is merely Wind inside me. Breathing in hope, breathing out love, adding my breath to the Wind, I share in the chorus of the Spirit. Then I open my eyes to see the leaves rustling, the grass bending, the living creation responding.

Your own connection to the Divine will surely differ.

---

1   Ephesians 6:18, Romans 8:26-27

3: The Good News

While all New Testament writers imagined they were on the cusp of the age of God's rule, they did not necessarily agree on the status of the Kingdom's arrival. Was it in part, in full, or still just around the corner? John's Gospel, as we discussed, presents a radically different picture from most other New Testament writings. It concludes that all promises have been delivered, and the new age has arrived in its entirely.

Given the disparity of beliefs among our Bible writers, it's no wonder Bible scholars today still argue about the nature and timing of Jesus' second coming. Small wonder that theologians today are embroiled in bitter arguments about the essence and existence of both heaven and hell. Small wonder that even our first church fathers, men who were the most familiar with the times and language of the New Testament, quarreled over the same things.

Perhaps all we can readily conclude from the Bible about eschatological matters is that the *aion* of God's messianic rule has begun. The Bible can't help us much with the matter of life after death, but it can help us figure out what's expected of us in this life.

Am I trying to disparage your own hope in an afterlife? No! Heavens, no! Jesus believed. Our belief in an afterlife can be a source of great comfort. I am merely pointing out that in the Gospels, afterlife teachings are ambiguous and tangential to Jesus' ministry. I am a Christian who *does not know* if there is life after death, and does not consider it a matter of relevance to my walk with Jesus.

But if the message of Jesus is not afterlife-oriented, what is it? What is the gospel that Jesus taught? The clearest answer may come from the Gospel of Luke:

So [Jesus] came to Nazareth, where he had been brought up. And as his custom was, he went into the synagogue on the Sabbath day, and stood

36   *The Good News*

up to read. **And he was handed the book of the prophet Isaiah. And when
he had opened the book, he found the place where it was written:**

**"The Spirit of the LORD is upon me, because he has anointed me to
preach the gospel to the poor; he has sent me to heal the brokenhearted,
to proclaim liberty to the captives and recovery of sight to the blind, to set
at liberty those who are oppressed; to proclaim the acceptable year of the
Lord."**

**Then he closed the book, and gave it back to the attendant and sat
down.**[1]

The word "gospel" means "good news." Jesus says his message
is good news—not to the prosperous, but to the poor. Not to the
happy, but to the brokenhearted. Not to the slave owner, but to
the captive. Not to the seeing, but to the blind. Jesus himself says
the reason he came was to "preach the acceptable year of the Lord."

Do you know what the "acceptable year of the Lord" is? Many
translations read "the year of the Lord's favor." Does that help explain it?

This special year, often called the Jubilee, occurs every fifty
years in the Old Testament. It is the year in which debts are forgiven, slaves are set free, and property is returned to its original
owner. It is a law that had fallen into disfavor, and it's anybody's
guess whether anyone at all observed the Jubilee year anymore by
Jesus' time. Having read these words about the Jubilee, Jesus tells
the crowd, "Today this scripture is fulfilled in your hearing."

Let's be clear, here. Jesus is not talking about proclaiming the
good news of a future resurrection. His gospel is not about heaven
at all. Jesus is talking about bringing relief for the desperate and
freedom for the oppressed, and this he calls the gospel. His message
is very this-worldly, and his gospel is directed to the commoner. The
same message is repeated a couple chapters later: "Blessed are you
who are poor."[2] Not "poor in spirit," but just plain "poor." Why?
Because, says Jesus, the Kingdom of God has arrived on earth, and
now things will be different.

---

1   Luke 4:16-20

2   Luke 6:20

The River of Life 37

You may be more familiar with Matthew's Sermon on the Mount than Luke's version, sometimes called the Sermon on the Plain. Both are basically the same scene, drawn from the same source. But in Luke's version, the sayings are very down to earth, not meant in a spiritual way at all. Let's look closer at the beatitudes.[1] In Luke, we're not dealing with the *poor in spirit,* we're dealing with the *poor.* We're not dealing with those who *hunger after justice,* but with those who are truly *hungry.* It's not about those who are persecuted *for righteousness' sake,* but simply all who are *persecuted.* Luke is not about spiritual needs, but about stark reality. In Luke, Jesus is concerned about those with empty stomachs, the real have-nots, the people who are weeping *now.*

Luke's Gospel has a different flavor from the very beginning. Consider again the "Hades" parable of Lazarus, the poor beggar sitting outside the gates of the rich man. This is not a story about right and wrong, but about haves and have-nots. The have-nots will be rewarded in the age to come, while the haves already have their reward. According to Luke, the only proper use of wealth is to give it to the poor. Where Matthew says, "do not lay up for yourselves treasure on earth," Luke is very specific in relating the same passage: "Sell your possessions and give alms." The Kingdom of God is not very good news for the rich and proud. In Luke, Jesus even presents money itself as evil, calling it "unrighteous mammon."[2]

To be fair, Jesus lived in a different time than we do. In a society skilled in surviving by the barter system, money had limited purpose. It was used to pay taxes, tolls, and tribute. It served as propaganda, being stamped with the image of the emperor—a horrid thing to devout Jews, who were taught that graven images were wrong. When Jesus was asked whether it was proper to pay tribute to Caesar, notice that he didn't even have a coin on him. He had to ask for one.

In this light, you can see how almost every connotation of money to urban Jews was negative. It represented political and religious control, in direct contrast to the prophets' dream of a

---

1   Luke 6:20-22
2   Luke 16:11

38   *The Good News*

world where everyone shared in God's earth and had plenty to eat
and drink.

So is Luke's version a more original peek into the true humanitarian ministry of Jesus? Here are Luke's beatitudes again:

> *Blessed are you poor, for yours is the Kingdom of God.*
> *Blessed are you who are hungry now, for you shall be satisfied.*
> *Blessed are you who weep now, for you shall laugh.*
> *Blessed are you when people hate and persecute you ... for behold, your*
> *reward is great in heaven.*

Which version more accurately reflects the desire of Jesus? Afterlife-oriented Christians naturally gravitate to Matthew's version.
What the poor really need, they insist, is the saving of their soul.
Their brief years of suffering on earth will soon be over and what
really matters is eternity. But liberal Christians lean toward Luke's
rendition. We can praise the "poor in spirit" some other day, they
insist. There are *real* poor people experiencing *real* hunger that need
our attention now!

So what did *Jesus* mean by this lecture? We'll probably be arguing about this as long as Christianity remains on the earth, but
if his proclamation of the Jubilee is any indication, Luke's version
gets the nod. The good news is that the marginalized in our midst
will no longer be ignored. You're not poor and oppressed, and have
no sympathy for those who are? Then maybe this isn't very good
news for you. Consider again the way Jesus taught us to pray: [1]

Your kingdom come. Your will be done on earth as it is in heaven.

Jesus is praying that God would finally come back and establish his righteous kingdom on earth. He pleads with God that
God's will would be done down here the way it is in up in heaven.

Give us this day our daily bread.

Very practical, isn't this? People need to eat. In the Kingdom
of God, everyone gets to eat, no one goes hungry. This is repeatedly
emphasized by the Old Testament prophets: there will one day be

---

1   Matthew 6:10-12

The River of Life 39

plenty of bread, and wine will flow in rivers. When Jesus staged the miraculous feeding of thousands, what we call the "loaves and fishes" miracle, he surely had this promise in mind. He was proving the Old Testament prophets right, and making a clear statement about the arrival of the messianic age.

Scholars continue to argue about what is meant by "daily bread." The Greek word translated into "daily" is *epiousios,* a word which appears nowhere else in scripture, and which must therefore be interpreted based upon the surrounding context or word construction. It may or may not mean "daily." Perhaps it means gluten-free. As long as we've been praying this prayer, we don't really know for sure what we're praying for. But here is what I think.

The story begins back in Exodus. When the Children of Israel escaped from Egypt, they grew hungry, and God fed them with miracle food. Manna. Daily bread from heaven, the "food of angels." So impressive was this daily bread that Jews in later centuries began to yearn for the bread of angels again. Many of the rabbis taught that in the age to come God would again provide bread from heaven. No one would ever go hungry.

When Jesus fed the multitude with loaves and fishes, they ate their fill but were unimpressed. They begged for a *real* miracle; they reminded Jesus that their fathers ate manna from heaven, not barley loaves and common fish. The wish for the messianic age to be ushered in with angel food was alive and well in Jesus' day.

Jesus had no angel food. He had only a small bit of common sustenance, which he happily shared. As it was passed from person to person, the provision didn't dwindle, it grew larger. Was the multitude contributing, learning to share, adding to the basket from their own belongings so that all could be fed? That would certainly be consistent with the teachings of Jesus. I don't know how everyone was fed, but I know that communal sharing would be no less a miracle.

Which brings us back to the prayer of Jesus. Give us this day our *epiousios* bread. Some scholars suggest the word means "for the current time." Others interpret it as "for the coming day." Still others read it as "for existence." But if you break the word up into its two main parts, *epi* means "above," and *ousia* means "substance." Putting them together renders something akin to "God-given substance." It is, I believe, a direct reference to the messianic era's anticipation of divine food, the daily provision from God. It turns out to be loaves and fishes, shared from person to person. God was in that multitude.

Christians who utter this prayer are begging for the realization of God's rule, when all people will live in harmony and all will be filled.

And forgive us our debts, as we forgive our debtors.

Don't fall into the trap of reading this verse spiritually. It too is a very down to earth request, for real people with real struggles. We must remember the climate of first-century peasantry, where debt was a serious foe, ranking up there with food and shelter. If a person fell into debt, he would most likely lose his land or wind up in indentured servitude (temporary slavery). Thus when Jesus came proclaiming the year of the Jubilee, the year when all debts are forgiven, he was referring directly and literally to releasing people's burden of debt.

It's common to read the Lord's Prayer like this: *Forgive us our sins, as we forgive the sins of others.* But this is a blatant mistranslation. Those who fall into debt aren't sinners, they are merely unfortunates. So where do heaven and hell fit into all this? Where is the reward for the righteous? Well, maybe we just aren't supposed to get so hung up on reward and punishment. Jesus described his mission on earth quite plainly, and it was not to steer people into a pleasant afterlife. His mission was to change this world. Therefore, perhaps what Christians should most be concerned about is helping Jesus build the Kingdom of God here on earth that he envisioned.

So let's talk about this Kingdom of God and what Jesus had in mind. Remember, even though Matthew called it the "Kingdom of Heaven," this kingdom isn't up in the sky. The kingdom comes down *from* heaven to earth, and it happened in the first century. It is a heavenly kingdom on earth. The arrival of the Kingdom of

The River of Life 41

Heaven is the fulfillment of the prophetic promises that God would once again take an active stance in the governance of earth.

If it helps, you may imagine the picture Revelation gives us of a glorious city (the New Jerusalem) descending from heaven to earth. Yes, in the Bible, this city floats down out of the heaven and settles on earth.[1] In this confusing vision, Jesus governs the world from his throne in the center of this new heavenly city.

So where is the "good news" in this story? Is it really such a beneficial thing when a world leader is appointed? Does it really matter whether or not this new ruler is the appointed Messiah, the representative of God? The prophets certainly thought so.

Isaiah prophesied that in this coming kingdom, the wolf will live with the lamb, the leopard will lie down with the goat, the calf and the lion will coexist; and a little child will lead them.[2]

Micah promised that God's temple will be exalted above the mountains, and people will stream to it from the nations. God will gather even the lame, everyone will sit under their own vine and their own fig tree, and none will be afraid.[3]

Jeremiah said that as the nations stream to the city of God, they will stand in awe, and tremble at the abundant peace and prosperity of God's provision.[4]

Amos said the crops will be so plentiful that the reapers will not be finished gathering the harvest before the plowman comes the next year to till the fields.[5]

There is, sadly, a downside. Before any of this could happen, according to Ezekiel, Israel must go through the fire.

Moreover the word of the Lord came to me, saying, "And you, son of man, thus says the Lord God to the land of Israel: 'An end! The end has come upon the four corners of the land. Now the end has come upon you, And I will send my anger against you; I will judge you according to your ways,

---

1   See Revelation 3:12 and 20:16. This matches the Jewish book of Jubilees, in which a New Jerusalem floats down from heaven to replace the old Jerusalem.

2   Isaiah 11:6

3   Micah chapter 4

4   Jeremiah 33:9

5   Amos 9:13

42   *The Good News*

and I will repay you for all your abominations. My eye will not spare you,
nor will I have pity; but I will repay your ways, and your abominations will
be in your midst; then you shall know that I am the Lord!'"[1]

Many other scriptures promise similar woes. In Leviticus 26,
God threatens Israel with the sword of their enemies, disease, pestilence, famine, and death. In Deuteronomy 32, the Song of Moses,
God foretells the final days of Israel, warning that he will bring
his arrows upon them, that the sword will destroy them, and that
pestilence and famine will overwhelm them. In Jeremiah 5, the
prophet threatens Judah with pestilence, famine, the sword, and
the arrow. The Day of the Lord would be terrible, indeed.

It matters not that these writers were surely referring to events
of their own day. Biblical writings were interpreted typologically,
cyclically, and in the minds of Jews in Jesus' day, they surely referred
as strongly to them as to those hundreds of years beforehand. The
next "Day of the Lord" would be even grander, even more terrible;
it would be the *real* Day, the one to usher in the *real* messianic age.

These grand expectations of a time of abundance, coupled
with the promise of first a period of God's wrath, led many Jews in
Jesus' day to misunderstand his message. Perhaps thinking they had
already survived the fury of the Lord, since they were already living
as a conquered people under the thumb of the Roman Empire, they
were now ready for a glorious military uprising. At any moment,
they expected God to send a messianic warrior to raise the Jews to
their rightful place above all other nations. The Kingdom of God
would be in control once again, enforced with a rod of iron, with
Israel at its center. Thus they could not grasp the grassroots message
of this backwoods prophet named Jesus:

Now when [Jesus] was asked by the Pharisees when the Kingdom of
God would come, he answered them and said, "The Kingdom of God does
not come with observation; nor will they say, 'See here!' or 'See there!' For
indeed, the Kingdom of God is within you."[2]

---

1   Ezekiel 7:1-4
2   Luke 17:20-21

The River of Life 43

Jesus insisted that the promised salvation had already arrived, it was right in the middle of them, and was theirs for the grasping. Let's talk about salvation, then. There's much written in the Bible about salvation. Everybody wants to be saved. But what are we actually saved from? Most Christians, when talking about salvation, have a picture in their heads about being rescued from a lost eternity. Salvation equates to heaven, in their minds.

You may be surprised to learn that whenever the Bible talks about salvation, it is talking about a rescue from something in this life. There are a few verses that speak of saving us from "the wrath to come," but it's a dubious assumption that they relate to the afterlife. Here are some examples:

"Brood of vipers! Who warned you to flee from the wrath to come?" (Said by John the Baptist)[1]

Much more then, being now justified by his blood, we shall be saved from wrath through him. (Written by Paul to the Romans)[2]

And to wait for his Son from heaven, whom he raised from the dead, even Jesus, which delivered us from the wrath to come. (Written by Paul to the Thessalonians)[3]

By now, you should recognize that Paul and John the Baptist were talking about the upcoming war. One consequence of God introducing a new messianic order was the violent overthrow of the older Mosaic order—abolishing the temple and its sacrifices. Why should we imagine that the "wrath to come" refers to the destruction of Jerusalem? Because other scriptures tell us clearly that Jesus warned of Jerusalem's pending carnage:

Then Jesus went out and departed from the temple, and his disciples came up to show him the buildings of the temple. And Jesus said to them, "Do you not see all these things? Assuredly, I say to you, not one stone shall be left here upon another, that shall not be thrown down."[4]

---

1 Matthew 3:7
2 Romans 5:9
3 1 Thessalonians 1:10
4 Matthew 24:1-2

44 *The Good News*

Forty years later, the Romans toppled the temple.

"Or those eighteen on whom the tower in Siloam fell and killed them, do you think that they were worse sinners than all other men who dwelt in Jerusalem? I tell you, no; but unless you repent you will all likewise perish."[1]

Forty years later, the residents of Jerusalem (save for the Christians, who escaped to Pella[2]) were besieged and slaughtered.

And while the crowds were thickly gathered together, [Jesus] began to say, "This is an evil generation. It seeks a sign, and no sign will be given to it except the sign of Jonah the prophet."[3]

Do you know what the sign of Jonah is? Perhaps you're familiar with this saying from the Gospels of Matthew and Luke. The "sign of Jonah" is that Jonah spent three days and three nights in the belly of the whale ... like Jesus spent three days in the grave, right?

Not according to Luke. He explains this saying in the next verse:

For as Jonah became a sign to the Ninevites, so also the Son of Man will be to this generation.[4]

As Luke explains, Jonah preached repentance to a wicked city. In Nineveh's case, the wicked city repented, and was saved. But in Jerusalem's case, there was no repentance, and Jerusalem perished. Forty years later—a biblical generation—it was completely leveled by the Romans.

One day, Jesus told a parable about wicked husbandmen.[5] A man planted a vineyard and left on a journey, leaving the vineyard in the care of tenants. At the time of harvest, he sent a servant to

---

1   Luke 13:4-5

2   "The whole body, however, of the church at Jerusalem, having been commanded by a divine revelation, given to men of approved piety there before the war, removed from the city, and dwelt at a certain town beyond the Jordan, called Pella." (Eusebius, Ecclesiastical History, Book 3, Chapter 5)

3   Luke 11:29

4   Luke 11:30

5   Mark 12:1-12; Matthew 21:33-46; Luke 20:9-19

The River of Life   45

collect some of the produce from the vineyard, but the tenants beat him and sent him away empty-handed. The vineyard owner sent another, and him they killed. He sent more, and some they beat, some they killed. Last of all, he sent his own son. But the tenants said to themselves, "This is the heir. Let us kill him, and the vineyard will be ours." So this they did. What then will the owner of the vineyard do? He will come, and put the tenants to death, and give the vineyard to others.

Matthew's Gospel says this parable was directed to "the chief priests and the Pharisees." Luke records that it was told to "the scribes and chief priests." Unfazed, the tenants of Jerusalem killed the Son of God anyway.

So God killed them, and gave Jerusalem to others.

The story of Jesus weeping over Jerusalem is worth revisiting:

Now as [Jesus] drew near, he saw [Jerusalem] and wept over it, saying, "If you had known, even you, especially in this your day, the things that make for your peace! But now they are hidden from your eyes. For days will come upon you when your enemies will build an embankment around you, surround you and close you in on every side, and level you, and your children within you, to the ground; and they will not leave in you one stone upon another, because you did not know the time of your visitation."[1]

Then Jesus trekked mournfully down the Mount of Olives to deliver his message of destruction to God's city. Forty years later, Jerusalem was destroyed precisely as predicted. Jesus' warning about *Gehenna* came to pass. If Jesus saw himself as the Son of Man, he may also have taken instruction from Old Testament scripture:

Son of man, set your face toward Jerusalem, preach against the holy places, and prophesy against the land of Israel.[2]

We now understand why it is only Jesus in the Bible who spoke of Gehenna, and only to a Palestinian audience. Neither Peter nor Paul, who preached to gentiles outside Jerusalem, mentioned Gehenna. This is because it has nothing to do with today's concept

---

1   Luke 19:41-44
2   Ezekiel 21:2

The Good News

of hell. It is not you or I that need to worry about the wrath to come. It is the Judeans, and their day of suffering came and went. God's wrath, as in Old Testament passages, has nothing to do with postmortem torture.

So what does salvation mean for us? Where is the good news, if we need not worry about being saved from God's wrath?

Here are a few things we are saved from:

1. A pointless, hopeless life.[1]
2. This present evil age.[2]
3. Fear of death.[3]
4. Our present alienation from God and need of reconciliation.[4]
5. Bondage to sin.[5]

Let's look at this list in more detail. Why do we need rescuing from a pointless, hopeless life? What does Paul mean, for example, when he says Jesus "gave himself for our sins, that he might deliver us from this present evil *aion*?" Does he mean Jesus died so that we could be raptured away from this evil world into heaven?

Certainly not. The answer lies in deciphering that confusing word *aion* again. *Aion* refers to "an age," and *aionios* means "belonging to that age." So what age is Paul talking about?

The Jews believed there were two ages of importance; the "present evil age" and the messianic age to come. Paul is telling his readers that Jesus' death, in some manner, is transitioning them from the old age to the new. Paul is insisting to his audience 2,000 years ago that the messianic age is breaking into the world. They are being delivered from the evil age. As Paul explains,

Therefore, if anyone is in Christ, he is a new creation; old things have passed away; behold, all things have become new.[6]

---

1   Ephesians 2:12

2   Galatians 1:4

3   Hebrews 2:15

4   2 Corinthians 5:19-20

5   Matthew 1:21, among many

6   2 Corinthians 5:17

The River of Life   47

How did Jesus' death rescue us from the old age? According to Paul, it was by atoning for our sins and reconciling us to God. The prophets promised that in the new age, God would return to earth and dwell with his people. Jesus made this possible. The pointless, hopeless life of the prior age is over.

We note, then, that all items on the above list are this-worldly. Salvation, in every instance in the Bible, means making life better *on this side of the grave.* Now, please understand. I am not denying the possibility of an afterlife. I am not denying that the Bible occasionally talks about life after death. I am saying that salvation as described in the Bible is earthly. God's gifts are to be enjoyed now. Jesus' vision of a God-ruled kingdom relates to this world. Our emphasis as Christians should not be for eternity, but for today. Afterlife-oriented Christians who live with their faces tilted heavenward dreaming of being whisked away from their troubles are missing the point of what it means to be a Christian.

4: THE HISTORICAL JESUS

Given the intended emphasis on life this side of the grave, our interest should be piqued all the more to learn what Jesus was really like, how he lived, and what he wanted from us. More than once, a reviewer of one of my books commented that I "subscribe to the historical Jesus school of thought." At first, this puzzled me a bit. Doesn't every Christian believe Jesus was a historical figure? That he was a flesh-and-blood person?

Their concern is that many scholars who pursue the quest for the historical Jesus do so without the burden of belief. There is no presumption among such scholars that the Jesus of history is the same person as the Christ of faith. That the Jesus before Easter is the same as the Jesus after Easter. After all, why would any scholar try to uncover the real Jesus if he believes Jesus is already properly represented in Christian tradition?

Liberal Christians see the other side of the coin. Wouldn't it be best to tweak our current-day beliefs about Jesus to match the person he really was? In one of my favorite verses in the Bible, we find this casual description of Jesus and how he lived:

God anointed Jesus of Nazareth with the Holy Spirit and with power, who went about doing good and healing all who were oppressed by the devil, for God was with him.[1]

I love this reminder about our chosen Messiah. He was a man who went around doing good. Perhaps more than any verse in the Bible, this memory captures the essence of the historical Jesus for me. This does little, however, to explain *why* Jesus did what he did. What was his motivation? What did he believe? What did he teach?

---

1 Acts 10:38

Now, as I lead into the topic of how Jesus lived and died, please don't think I'm dictating a particular theology of the cross, or a particular meaning of the words Messiah or Savior, or how you must picture the devil, or even how you must imagine God. I will speak in religious language without apology, just as I did earlier about Jesus' resurrection, because such topics deserve a higher plane of discussion, but I am not trying to dictate your religious beliefs.

So here we go. Here is a man so open to incarnation, so infused with the Spirit of God, that he in time came to be recognized as divine. When we dig beneath our religion to the historical Jesus, we uncover a man who preached the beginning of the age of God's rule. In other words, he strove toward his picture of what this world would be like if God were king. Jesus believed everyone should be able to enjoy God's glorious creation. He taught how that could be accomplished, through compassion and understanding. He performed the expected miracles as proof that the messianic age had arrived. It is a shame if we refuse to acknowledge this new age, and pretend it still resides in our future. Rather than sharing in its joy, we tend to hijack Jesus' message and turn it into an afterlife-oriented religion, redirecting our purpose from the Kingdom of God on earth to a dream of floating away above the clouds. That was never the vision of the Jesus who walked this earth 2,000 years ago.

Of primary importance to Jesus' vision is recognizing that things will be different now that the Messiah has arrived and the Kingdom has begun. The Jews dreamed of the day when God would come back and take an active part in guiding humanity, and Jesus did just that. He brought God back. The Jews longed for the day when the Spirit would once again be felt, and Jesus dispensed the Spirit. The Jews taught that there would be a time of great suffering between the two ages—they called this period the "Woes of the Messiah"—and Jesus, surely drawing inspiration from Isaiah's depiction of a suffering servant, took God's wrath upon himself and died in our place on the cross so the new age could begin.[1] The Jews expected their Messiah to deliver a new law for the new age,

---

1   In early Christian thinking, Jesus' death apparently did not atone for the Jews who rejected him, so the destruction of Jerusalem remained necessary.

The River of Life   51

so Jesus did. As Moses brought the first law down the mountain
from God, so did Jesus stand on a mountain and deliver a new law.
Over and over, Jesus repeated the refrain "You have heard it said
... but I say ...." Here is an example:

**You have heard that it was said, 'You shall love your neighbor and hate
your enemy.' But I say to you, love your enemies.** [1]

If you're wondering where his audience heard such things,
the answer is in the Synagogue. These rules come straight out of
the Law: the Old Testament. In other words, Jesus felt it was per-
missible to say "The scripture says this, but I say this." Espousing
a higher standard than scripture, Jesus called his followers to step
up to the next level, for the new era. We, too, would do well to
take this advice, if we ever find scripture to be contradictory to the
Kingdom.

The Law divided between the clean and the unclean, listing
a number of abnormalities from dwarfs to hunchbacks to homo-
sexuals to blind people to lame people and calling such people
abominations [2] so as to exclude them from approaching the altar in
the Temple. Got a smashed nose? You're out in the cold. Missing
a finger? Forget about it, you're damaged goods. Many Jews in the
first century still considered such people less than perfect, but Jesus
waved it all away. Quit judging, he said. Things are going to be different now, he insisted. The prophets—especially Isaiah—dreamed
of the day a messiah would arrive to bring equality, healing the
abominations. The blind would see, the deaf would hear, the lame
would walk. Everyone would be allowed in the new temple. There
would be no segregation for those different from the rest. One day,
Jesus grew so angry that he strode into the temple and overturned
the tables of the money changers and the vendors selling sacrificial

---

1   Matthew 5:43-44

2   The Bible does not specifically list the blind and lame as abominations, it
merely associates them as such. The word abomination, while it sounds horrid
in today's language, described a number of seemingly innocuous differences and
imperfections throughout Leviticus and Deuteronomy.

52   *The Historical Jesus*

animals. John's Gospel says he drove the animals (and perhaps the
vendors!) away with a whip. And then ...

**... Then the blind and the lame came to him in the temple, and he
healed them.**[1]

He didn't heal them all, of course. Jesus healed a few that he
came in contact with, and accepted the rest. The age of abominations is past and a new era is beginning. In this age, anyone who
wishes may share in the greatness of God's creation. In this age, it
is the meek, the merciful, the pure in heart, the peacemakers who
will be blessed. Here's how we turn earth back into Eden, Jesus said,
as he stood on a mountain delivering God's new rules:

- Do not hide your candle under a bushel anymore.[2]
- Drop your hostilities.[3]
- Do not lust after that which belongs to another.[4]
- If a man takes your coat, give him your cloak as well.[5]
- Honor your responsibility to those who depend on you.[6]
- Love even your enemies.[7]
- Give secretly.[8]
- Pray that the age of God's rule will be a success.[9]
- Forgive.[10]
- Do not think of yourself. Do not worry about tomorrow.
  God will provide.[11]
- Do not judge.[12]

---

1   Matthew 21:14
2   Matthew 5:15-16
3   Matthew 5:22-24
4   Matthew 5:28
5   Matthew 5:40
6   Matthew 5:31-32
7   Matthew 5:44
8   Matthew 6:1-4
9   Matthew 6:10
10 Matthew 6:14-15
11 Matthew 6:25-31
12 Matthew 7:1-2

The River of Life   53

- And do not imagine you can be a participant in the new age without doing these things. [1]

The Jews had a different idea of how God would usher in the new age—they dreamed of a military savior patterned after the warrior David, who would subdue the nations under his feet and elevate the Jews as God's chosen people once again—but Jesus blew that idea away. Call it a paradigm shift if you prefer. This kingdom will be a grassroots operation, he insisted, starting like a pinch of leaven in a loaf of bread, destined to expand and permeate the whole loaf. Like a mustard seed, the smallest of seeds, which grows into a tree. God will be here with us to help. The Spirit will guide us, and together we will make it happen.

This is the Jesus who walked the earth 2,000 years ago.

Curiously, however, traditional Christian beliefs often preclude careful examination of the historical Jesus. Part of the problem, I think, is that we want to believe the New Testament was written for us. It wasn't. It was written for first-century readers with first-century issues. Jesus cannot be understood outside the context of first-century Judaism, nor can the New Testament be understood if removed from its backdrop of the Jerusalem war, which put a violent end to Judaic customs and sent confused Palestinians scuttling in every direction.

Hand-in-hand with understanding the historical Jesus is grasping the purpose and method of the evangelists who recorded his story. Consider this: All of our four Gospels were written anonymously. We don't know who wrote any of them or where they were written, except that they were written in Greek ... not Hebrew or Aramaic, as we would expect. In the second century, our church fathers began to make claims about the authorship of these anonymous Gospels. Stories surfaced about authorship and the consensus grew that Matthew, a tax collector and one of the Twelve original disciples, wrote the first gospel; Mark, a disciple of Peter, penned the second; Luke, who was a companion to Paul, wrote the third;

---

1   Matthew 7:21

and finally, an apostle named John, one of the inner three of Jesus' entourage, penned the fourth in his old age.

But these claims about authorship introduce more questions than they answer. Commonly called the Synoptic Problem, the books of Matthew, Mark and Luke (known as the Synoptics, a word which means "in agreement") are so similar that it is impossible that they could be independent testimonies. Moreover, they appear to be written later than our patristic fathers claim. This is far too complex a topic for this short booklet to address in detail, but most scholars agree that Mark was the first gospel written, with Mathew and Luke copying from Mark. Half of the verses in Mark reappear in Luke, and 90% reappear in the Matthew, often word-for-word.

Mark appears to have been completed around 70 CE, just as the war was nearing its end, with Matthew a decade or so later. Most scholars date Luke to about the time of Matthew, though some argue for the early second century. John, usually considered the final gospel written, joins the rest at about 95 CE. Thus, all were written in the shadow of the most horrific war in Israel's history up to that time. This war, thought to be a covenantal destruction promised by God, with its advance prediction by Jesus and his followers, greatly influenced Christian thought. For example, if you find that Matthew focuses more graphically on "hell" (the destruction of Jerusalem) than the other three gospels, that is to be expected; this is probably the first gospel to be completed after the war, and some scholars surmise that its author was displaced from Judea by the war.

So now we have a chronological order. If we order the gospels by date with first Mark, then Matthew, Luke, and finally John, an unmistakable trend surfaces. Jesus becomes more and more supernatural as time goes on. Or, more to the point for us, Jesus becomes more and more human as we step backward in time. In John's Gospel, written near the end of the first century, Jesus is in full control, portrayed as God himself. But by the time we reach back to Mark's Gospel, Jesus is quite human. Mark knows nothing about a virgin birth, but portrays Jesus as estranged from his family, disowning mother and brothers, hardly an endorsement for the idea

The River of Life   55

of Mary being informed by an angel of Jesus' divinity. Once Jesus' ministry begins, he sometimes fails as he tries to heal others, or requires a second effort.[1] At the end of his life, Jesus cries in agony from the cross, distressed over how it all ended: "My God, my God, why have you forsaken me?" Is it safe to say that as we read earlier and earlier writings, we get closer to the historic Jesus?

Going back even further to the writings of Paul (who was our first New Testament writer), we find no trace of Jesus' miracles, no virgin birth, no physical resurrection. Instead, Paul presents Jesus as a man born quite naturally, "born of a woman under the law" and "according to the flesh," in the lineage of King David.[2] Paul's *adoptionist* theology is stated quite plainly in his letter to the Romans, where he writes that Jesus became the Son of God at the time he was raised from the dead; not before.[3] Paul presents the resurrected Jesus not in a physical body walking the earth, but rather as a light from heaven ... a spiritual being like God, seeable only by believers.

Might there be evidence of Christian writings even before the time of Paul? Scholars propose a hypothetical document they've titled "Q," meaning "source," which served as a common source of Jesus' sayings for the writers of Matthew and Luke. The evidence for this document is very strong, but scholars disagree on when it was written. We know for sure only that it had to come before the gospels of Matthew and Luke. In Q, Jesus is more of a sage than a savior, he performs no miracles, and his resurrection goes unmentioned.

We could also examine what is known about James, the brother of Jesus. Perhaps a sibling can carry us all the way back to the real Jesus. James was immediately appointed to be the elder of the church in Jerusalem, the mother church of first-century Christianity. He became the top guy in the whole shebang after Jesus died. So what does James have to say?

---

1   Mark 6:5-6 8:22-25;

2   See Romans 1:3 and Galatians 4:4. For an idea of how this phrase "born of a woman" was understood, see Job 1:1, 15:14, 25:4

3   Romans 1:3-4

56   *The Historical Jesus*

The Ebionite sect was probably the first established Christian church in Jerusalem,[1] and therefore founded by James, so unless their doctrine quickly became distorted after James's death, what we know of their later beliefs may help us uncover what James taught. They focused on a works-based mission, and held James in very high regard after his martyrdom. This church did not ascribe divinity to Jesus nor did they believe in the virgin birth. They were, like John and Paul, "adoptionists," believing Jesus became the "Son of

---

1   Based on several recent studies into Jewish Christianity, the most likely scenario in my mind for the emergence of the Ebionites runs like this: The Pella Tradition—the story of Christians escaping from the Roman siege of Jerusalem in 70 AD, as told by Church Fathers Eusebius and Epiphanius and as reported in Luke chapter 21—is true, and a large portion of the Jerusalem Christians relocated to Pella. These early Christians were most commonly known as the Nazarenes. They observed Torah Law, as per the compromise reached with Paul at the Jerusalem Council. (See Acts 15 and Galatians 2.) In this compromise, Jewish Christians held true to Mosaic Law while Gentile Christians were freed from such restrictions. In the early second century, a schism occurred among these Christians over Christology. One faction retained the name Nazarenes and aligned themselves closely with Gentile Christianity, which had become the orthodox position. The other faction eschewed Christ's divinity, remained distrustful of Paul's teachings, and became known as the Ebionites, or the "Poor Ones."

Which of these two sects more closely aligned with the original Jewish Christians in Jerusalem? Most scholars cite a lack of evidence that early Jewish Christians differed in Christological view from the mainstream Church, and therefore side with the Nazarenes. But to me, this lack of tension proves just the opposite: Jewish Christianity probably evolved alongside the developing ideas of Gentile Christianity, and the Bible itself betrays how Christology evolved in the first century. Earlier Christians, both Jew and Gentile, understood the Messiahship of Jesus in less divine ways. But given Paul's harsh conflict with these Jerusalem Christians (whom scholars have labeled the "Judaizers") over Judaic customs, I would give the nod to the Ebionite teaching as more original, since they preserve the friction felt between Paul and Jerusalem.

The Ebionites, then, are most likely a Jewish Christian sect which worshipped alongside the developing gentile church, but who experienced a "back to Jesus" schism in the early second century, being unable to stomach the trend toward high Christology and focusing instead on good works, Torah observance and poverty.

The River of Life 57

God" at his baptism (or, as Paul believed, after his resurrection)—
no surprise I suppose, if the brother of Jesus himself was its founder.

Some critical scholars, such as A. T. Robinson in *Redating the New Testament,* propose that the epistle of James, attributed to the brother of Jesus, actually was penned by his very hand. It does indeed mirror Ebionite thinking, unmystical, ethical and practical, teaching a works-based salvation. The Historical Jesus probably emphasized a much more this-worldly, works-based message than many Christians prefer to believe.

This begs the question, then. Would Jesus want us to bathe in grace, just believing and enjoying, or would he rather we share in supporting the messianic age by following his example?

Now, I'm sure this foray into the historical Jesus leaves many readers feeling ungrounded, but may I restate again that it is not my intention to destroy anyone's faith. I happen to find the earlier writers' human portrayal of Jesus more inspiring, and completely understand how they could revere Jesus *as the Messiah* for his works and humanitarian teachings. They shared his dream and unrelenting drive to inaugurate the Kingdom of God, even though these same Christians often disagreed on the nature of Jesus and his resurrection. For such an extraordinary man, his life and teachings were enough. This by no means implies that later writers, who sought to uncover deeper truths about Jesus' divinity and place within the Godhead, were *wrong*. Of such truths I cannot speak, for I am no good at believing. Yet I share with believers a great admiration, respect, and spiritual dependency upon the Jesus who lived before the Resurrection.

My point is merely this: the beliefs you and I hold are no more diverse than those of the first Christians, the men closest in time to Jesus himself. Perhaps the particulars of our beliefs should not be allowed to separate us. Perhaps the example of Jesus should instead bring us together.

Deeds, not creeds.

5: Doing Our Part

The kingdom Jesus envisioned is very earthy. It is shared by people in this world making life better for people in this world. So who do you suppose gets to share in the Kingdom of God?

If we pose this question to Jesus, we might get a surprising answer. Here is a list of people who we know Jesus and the Twelve associated with:

- Tax collectors (people of ill repute).

- Lepers (social outcasts).

- Prostitutes (sinners).

- The lame and blind (physically challenged).

- The poor (people who cannot return our favor).

- Ethiopians and Nigerians (people of different nationality and race).

- Eunuchs and same-sex partners (people of different sexual orientation).[1]

- Slaves (people below us in caste).

---

1 No, I'm not kidding. First, eunuchs: *He that is wounded in the stones, or hath his privy member cut off, shall not enter into the congregation of the LORD.* –*Deuteronomy 23:1*. But Philip baptized a eunuch (Acts 8:36). Second, same-sex partners: *Thou shalt not lie with mankind, as with womankind: it is abomination.* –*Leviticus 18:22*. But Matthew 8:5-13 and Luke 7:1-10 tell of Jesus healing a centurion's servant who is dying. The Greek word used for "servant" is "pais," which many scholars convincingly argue implies a young male lover. The context of the verse supports this conclusion, so Jesus may have condoned a same-sex relationship.

60   *Doing Our Part*

- Samaritans (people of different religious persuasion).

If we believe that the influence of the Kingdom is world-wide—that God is king of the world in this age—then it's hard to think of anybody outside the Kingdom who doesn't want to be outside. Of all of the people Jesus accepted, the category listed last on the above list most intrigues me. It may be counterintuitive to say that the Kingdom of God is not a religious construction, but it is not. That Jesus included God in the picture should not surprise us, nor does it present a religious claim. Jesus lived in a different culture than today, in ancient Jerusalem and rural Palestine, where God's existence and participation in world events was simply a given. Supernatural intervention was the norm, with supernatural beings as the movers and shakers. The Kingdom was not a religious statement, for "religion" as we know it is a more recent develop-ment. Instead, the Kingdom Jesus envisioned was a humanitarian movement, a way of life, a vision for a better world, a philosophical stance that affirms all people as respectable, equal, and loved. It is the result of God being king, and that is why the Kingdom tran-scends unexpected borders.

It's true that Jesus couched his movement in religious terms, calling it the Kingdom of God. He knew no more acute means of highlighting that this was indeed a climactic, world-changing effort than to tie it explicitly to the promise of the prophets of Israel. Jesus was, after all, a Jew. He also felt convinced that his Kingdom vision was the will of God for mankind. Of this I'm sure.

Nevertheless, many liberal Christians struggle to imagine Jesus' vision in religious terms. Much of today's Christianity, we liberals insist, is an unnecessary belief system others have built atop Jesus' message. One of the walls Jesus specifically broke down was the wall of religious intolerance, when he spent so much time defending and enjoying those devil-deceived Samaritans without attempting to convert them. He wanted only for them to share in the Kingdom.

One day, Jesus' disciples came to him distraught that anoth-er person they didn't know was baptizing people in Jesus' name. Couldn't he make him stop? Jesus' answer was that the man was not

The River of Life 61

against him, so he must be on Jesus' side. The fellow was helping to grow the Kingdom and should not be deterred. In fact, there is only one "religion" that Jesus ever condemned. One worship that is unquestionably wrong. It is the worship of money.[1]

While religions divide people, the Kingdom of God binds us together, minimizing our differences and emphasizing our equality. (Do be aware that the Bible does not promise equality in the sense that all people will share the same privileges, but that all are equally loved by God and equally accepted in the Kingdom.)

I could go on finding more equals the way I started out this chapter, but it's a dreary exercise. It's much more fun excluding people than including them, right? So who do we get to kick out of the Kingdom, according to Jesus?

The answer, of course, is Pharisees. These people were the ultra-religious of Jesus' day, whose righteous standards and strict laws prevented them from accepting any of the above classes of people. The simple answer to who is excluded from the Kingdom is this: anyone who would in their righteousness exclude someone else.

But what about sin? Doesn't Christianity have something to do with Jesus dying to save us from our sin? We surely can't accept just anybody unless they change their ways, right? Paul, for example, was much stricter than Jesus. His letter to the Corinthians excludes a number of baddies, some of whom I'd happily befriend but others I'd feel a little nervous being around.[2] Yet it's not my preferences that matter, is it? It's Jesus, not me or Paul, whom we take as our example.

One thing I noticed very early as I was researching for my book about the Gospel of John is that there is no condemnation in that gospel for the sinner. As renowned Johannine scholar Raymond E. Brown points out, "The Fourth Gospel is notably deficient on precise moral teaching when compared with the synoptic gospels." No sins of behavior are listed in John, only the sin of unbelief, and the only belief that matters is whether we believe God has sent his Messiah to change the world. This is not to say that Jesus always

1   Matthew 6:24
2   1 Corinthians 6:9

62   *Doing Our Part*

approved of what he saw, but that condemnation was simply not his focus. The Jesus movement, at least according to this gospel, is simply not about right and wrong. It is about life. Abundant life, better than we can imagine. *Aionios life.*

But do you think this will happen without our help? Will God simply snap his fingers and turn everything to gold? I assure you, it will not happen without effort, nor did Jesus imagine that it could.

Then [Jesus] said to his disciples, "The harvest truly is plentiful, but the laborers are few. Therefore pray the Lord of the harvest to send out laborers into his harvest."[1]

We are put to work with Jesus. I love the analogy of the harvest field. After all, in the messianic age, we are promised that everyone will have plenty to eat. Brilliant, this analogy is, reminding us of the dream of feeding every mouth. So how do we become laborers for Jesus? How do we make earth more heaven-like, inching closer to the dream of a Kingdom of God?

Here is one way: Jesus taught by example and by parable that we should share our table with others. Jesus was a maverick; in his day, this simply wasn't done. A man of importance would never eat at a table with someone of lower status. Jesus, however, routinely broke with tradition, by which he was telling us the new age had arrived. Everyone would now be able to eat together as equals. He broke tradition in practice (and was condemned for eating with sinners and tax collectors), in miracles (once or twice he encouraged thousands to sit down together and share a God-given meal), and in ritual (the Eucharist). Remember, the nibble of bread and sip of wine we share today in church was originally celebrated as an entire meal, where the Christian community would gather and share together. Jesus wanted us to remember him in this manner: share your table with others as equals, all partaking of the same meal together. In a beautiful picture of universal humanity, he indicated that if we treat others in this neighborly fashion, it will be as if we are doing the same for him:

---

1   Matthew 9:37-38

The River of Life   63

For I was hungry and you gave me food; I was thirsty and you gave me drink; I was a stranger and you took me in; … Assuredly, I say to you, inasmuch as you did it to one of the least of these my brethren, you did it to me.[1]

But opening up our table to others is only the beginning. All Christians recognize that Jesus encouraged kindness and compassion. We read in Paul's letter to the Corinthians that love is the greatest of all gifts.[2] We read stories like *The Good Samaritan* and know that we're expected to spread kindness in the world. Conservative or liberal, we all know this is something Jesus emphasized, and we joyfully follow his example. Here is that example again:

God anointed Jesus of Nazareth with the Holy Spirit and with power, who went about doing good and healing all who were oppressed by the devil, for God was with him.[3]

Do you struggle to find devils today? I'm not advocating the demonology of first-century Judeo-Christianity, as in this verse. The New Testament was written in a time when virtually all people understood there to be a spiritual world ruled by good and evil spirits—angels and demons. One scholar counted 123 different demons identified by name in rabbinic literature.[4] Satan, the chief demon, they understood ruled over an army of evil angelic figures. Many Christians in third-world countries experience the same supernatural powers of light and darkness still today.

If you believe in invisible, extra-dimensional warfare between good and evil, you should have no trouble appreciating this verse. If you *don't* believe in demonology, that's wonderful … stay right where you're at. We seem to have conquered our demons in Western countries, chased them right away by shutting them out of our worldview, and if such creatures really do exist elsewhere, I see no value in restoring their foothold here in the West by returning to yesterday's belief system.

---

1   Matthew 25:35,40
2   See 1 Corinthians chapter 13
3   Acts 18:38
4   J. Maier, in *Reallexikon für Antike und Christentum*, vol. 9, cols. 680-87

64   *Doing Our Part*

Yet you need not think in terms of ancient demonology in order to recognize that there are harmful powers on earth greater than human strength. Here's an example: One of the foulest "demons" I've encountered is the overpowering dependency caused by alcohol and drugs. Someone battling a physical addiction can feel as powerless as if they were possessed by a demon! While you and I are totally incapable of healing another's addictions, we can certainly sympathize with anyone battling this disease, rather than stereotyping or marginalizing. Their struggle hardly deserves belittling. I think all Christians would agree with this.

But where liberals and conservatives most often disagree is whether or not this-worldly compassion is the *primary focus* of Jesus' teaching. We argue about whether this really is the gospel message, and whether it really is directed for the poor:

[God] has anointed me to preach the gospel to the poor; he has sent me to heal the brokenhearted, to proclaim liberty to the captives and recovery of sight to the blind, to set at liberty those who are oppressed; to proclaim the acceptable year of the Lord.[1]

We argue about what it is that Jesus commands us to do. I've heard it said that there really is very little specific direction given by Jesus, and in a sense this may be true. Faithful Jews obey over 600 Old Testament laws, but Mark's Gospel whittles the list down to just two: love God and love your neighbor. Surprisingly, John's Gospel drops the former, and tells us twice that our one command is to love one another. This, says Jesus, is the secret to *aionios* life.

But in another sense, Jesus gave us *plenty* to do, by word and example, if only we will quit "spiritualizing" his message to soften its blow. Perhaps we are unable or unwilling to fulfill Jesus' request to "sell all and give to the poor," but let us not pretend he didn't say it. Perhaps we struggle to forgive the debts others owe us, but let us not pretend it isn't the command of Jesus. The more I study the life and teachings of Jesus, putting them in first-century context, the more down to earth they become to me. Jesus' message, according

---

1   Luke 4:8

The River of Life   65

to the Gospel of Luke, is that the ultimate Jubilee has arrived. God is stepping in to set things right again on this earth.

The gospel message of Jesus has nothing to do with an afterlife. It has everything to do with clothing the naked, feeding the hungry, assisting the poor. It is through the lens of Jesus' dream for this earth—his promise that God has returned and the age of God's righteous rule is upon us—that liberal Christians examine social and political issues today. It is through Christ's vision that we weigh the pros and cons of issues such as health care, welfare programs, and green earth. It is with Jesus as our example that we fight against the marginalization of others, whether caused by race, religion, or sexual preference. Jesus, as best I can tell, never discriminated or felt any bigotry. His compassion extended to all who were marginalized. The reminder that God's age has begun guides our acceptance and love for all people.

Paradoxically, it is here where we liberal Christians most appreciate the hands-on approach of our brethren in conservative churches. Soup kitchens, shelters, medical missions, relief organizations, charitable aid societies, these things make for a better world. Nobody does it better than our Christian churches. Nobody brings us closer to the dream of Jesus.

If a common denominator can be found between liberal and conservative branches of Christianity, it is here that we can join hands and move forward, continuing the work Jesus began.

6: But What About Miracles?

Eight hundred years before Christ, these words were penned by the prophet Isaiah about the coming age of God's rule:

> Say to those who are fearful-hearted, "Be strong, do not fear! Behold, your God will come with vengeance, with the recompense of God; he will come and save you." Then the eyes of the blind shall be opened, and the ears of the deaf shall be unstopped. Then the lame shall leap like a deer, and the tongue of the dumb sing. For waters shall burst forth in the wilderness, and streams in the desert.[1]

Eight hundred years later, John the Baptist, demoralized and sitting in prison, sent word to Jesus asking if he was really God's Messiah; if the world was really changing as promised; or whether John's preaching had been in error. Jesus replied with these encouraging words:

> Jesus answered and said to them, "Go and tell John the things which you hear and see: The blind see and the lame walk; the lepers are cleansed and the deaf hear; the dead are raised up and the poor have the gospel preached to them.[2]

"Yes, John," says Jesus, "God has finally come back like Isaiah promised. The age of his rule has begun. The poor may finally rejoice."

But did Jesus really do miracles like Isaiah promised? I confess my own skepticism, yet current scholarly consensus accepts the healing stories of Jesus as often genuine. E. P. Sanders claims it to be an "almost indisputable" historical fact that "Jesus was a Galilean

---

1   Isaiah 35:4-6

2   Matthew 11:4-5

68   *But What About Miracles*

who preached and healed."[1] Through the use of historical-critical analysis, John P. Meier finds many of his miracles authentic.[2] Raymond Brown notes that "Scholars have come to realize that one cannot dismiss Jesus' miracles simply on modern rationalist grounds, for the oldest traditions show him as a healer."

So I must hesitantly acquiesce: Jesus inaugurated the age of God's rule by performing the promised healing miracles. He was the real deal.

At this point, I hear an objection. It's all fine and well to preach compassion for the poor in this age, but none of us can perform healing miracles like Jesus. We can't really continue the work Jesus began, can we?

Yes, we can, if we understand the *purpose* behind Jesus' miracles. While the Gospel writers were presenting the miracles of Jesus as evidence of the in-breaking of the messianic age, they were also pointing out how these miracles changed lives far beyond physical mending. Let me give you a few examples.

And behold, a leper came and worshiped him, saying, "Lord, if you are willing, you can make me clean." Then Jesus put out his hand and touched him, saying, "I am willing; be cleansed." Immediately his leprosy was cleansed.[3]

Then they came to him, bringing a paralytic who was carried by four men. And when they could not come near him because of the crowd, they uncovered the roof where he was. So when they had broken through, they let down the bed on which the paralytic was lying. When Jesus saw their faith, he said to the paralytic, "Son, your sins are forgiven you."[4]

Then he put his hands on his eyes again and made him look up. And he was restored and saw everyone clearly. Then he sent him away to his house …[5]

---

1   *Jesus and Judaism*, by Sanders, p. 11

2   *Marginal Jew*, 2:617-45

3   Matthew 8:2-4

4   Mark 2:3-5

5   Mark 8:25-26

The River of Life 69

A few things should stand out from these examples: First, while Jesus was only one of many healers in the first century, he was a very good one! His reputation shined! But perhaps the thing that most separated Jesus' healing miracles from the rest was that Jesus healed people for free. He did not consider it his career, but his gift from God to share.

Another thing that made Jesus' healing unique is that he focused as much on healing the soul as he did the body. He commonly accompanied his healings with the words "You are made clean," or "your sins are forgiven." Then he sent them home. Why? Because now they could rejoin their family, their village. No longer unclean, they could lift their eyes as equals to their comrades.

Physical deformations such as those suffered by the lame and blind, and sicknesses like leprosy, were recognized in Jesus' day as punishments from God for one's sins. Such obvious sinners were naturally rejected from the temple. They were outcasts, relegated to the edge of society, where their only hope of survival was to beg. People were taught to say, upon seeing such a sinner, "Praise God, who sees into the inner heart, and knows what they deserve." A person who sees a blind or lame person should praise God as the righteous judge, who "punishes the children for the sins of their fathers to the third and fourth generation."[1] So when Jesus pronounced these people clean and sent them home, he was insisting that they were to be restored to a respected place in society.

In John's Gospel, Jesus' disciples encounter a blind man, and they ask Jesus a question: "Master, who did sin, this man, or his parents, that he was born blind?" Jesus answers that it was neither, but rather the man was born blind to help demonstrate a point. This point, we learn near the end of the chapter, is that it is not this man who is blind, but the Pharisees who reject him. They cannot see that the man was never a sinner, never deserved to be an outcast in the first place.

In healing, then, Jesus removed the stigma of sin. He made people whole. And it was this—the forgiving of sins—which irritated the Jewish ruling body more than anything else. You see,

---

1   Exodus 20:5-6

forgiving sins and cleansing impurities was the temple's job. When you became unclean by any of a number of activities or mishaps, you took your money to the temple, paid exorbitant prices for a sacrifice, performed your duties before the priesthood, and supported the system. Then you were accepted back into society as cleansed. Unless, of course, your physical ailment made it clear that God still rejected you.

Do you know how to cleanse a leper? Here is how you do it, according to the temple.

Find a couple birds. Kill one in a vessel over running water. Dip the other one in the blood of the dead one. Sprinkle the dead bird's blood on the leper seven times, then let the live bird fly away. Wait for the leper to shave off all his hair, including his eyebrows. Make him bathe daily for a week. Tell him to come back with two spotless lambs and one spotless ewe. If they aren't spotless enough, make him buy new animals from the temple. Kill them all for a burnt offering. Wipe some of the ewe's blood on the leper's ear, thumb, and big toe. Go get some oil. Sprinkle him seven times with oil, again dobbing some of the oil on his ear, thumb, and toe. Do it once more. Then pour what's left of the oil over the leper's head. Finally, kill a couple doves. Offer one as a sin offering, and the other as a burnt offering.

Jesus did things differently:

Then Jesus, moved with compassion, stretched out his hand and touched him, and said to him, "I am willing; be cleansed."[1]

Jesus bypassed the system. I don't know which healing technique proved more effective, but Jesus' method differed. No shaving all your hair to mark yourself as different. No embarrassing public rituals. No expensive sacrifices. No pretention that you have sinned before God. Merely a compassionate touch and a gentle word: *Be clean.* In other words, *Yes, God loves you.*

Jesus cleansed even those too poor to appear in the temple. Even those with physical ailments proving they were rejected by God. He offered hope, acceptance, and respectability to all. In fact,

---

1   Mark 1:40-41

The River of Life 71

his ministry seemed to focus primarily on those who *needed* hope, acceptance, and respectability. Yes, Jesus healed people physically, but it seems to me that he did so by first healing them spiritually. Once they believed they were not sinners, rejected by God and by men, but equals, they were mentally prepared to participate in healing the body as well.

I'm not a neurologist, and I don't pretend to understand the intricacies of mind and body, how intertwined they are. I don't know the limits. I don't know how prayer, or positive attitude, or meditation, or belief in God, heals the body. I find it fascinating that it does, and that Jesus recognized this. He never once attributed his healing accomplishments to his own prowess, or even to the power of God. He instructed his recipients to merely believe, and his successes were attributed to their faith:

He said to the ruler of the synagogue, "Do not be afraid; only believe."[1]

Jesus said to him, "If you can believe, all things are possible to him who believes."[2]

And he said to her, "Daughter, your faith has made you well."[3]

Then Jesus said to him, "Go your way; your faith has made you well."[4]

Likewise, his rare failures seem predicated on the lack of faith:

Now he could do no mighty work there, except that he laid his hands on a few sick people and healed them. And he marveled because of their unbelief.[5]

Regardless of *how* Jesus healed, however, New Testament writers quickly grasped its hidden meaning. Israel longed for the day when God would confound the nations by again producing signs and wonders. Such miracles would be greater than those performed

---

1   Mark 5:36

2   Mark 9:23

3   Mark 5:34

4   Mark 10:52

5   Mark 6:5-6

72   *But What About Miracles*

by Moses. The Psalms proclaim this sad but hopeful state of mind: *We are given no miraculous signs; no prophets are left, and none of us knows how long this will be.*[1] Although there was disagreement between Jewish sects about whether or not the Messiah would himself perform miracles—some anticipated merely a military leader—the messianic age would definitely be accompanied by miracles.

Seeing Jesus' miracles, then, his followers reasoned he had to be the one. But more than this, the messianic age had to be beginning. The Gospel writers were making a very explicit claim in highlighting Jesus' miracles: the anticipated Messiah had arrived; the new age had begun; everything would now be different. Some New Testament writers anticipated a future return of Jesus after he ascended—a "second coming" on the clouds—and some did not, but *all* of them understood the messianic age to be beginning. It was absolutely beyond the comprehension of any of the Bible's writers that, after the Messiah came, it would be yet another 2,000 years before the age of God's rule would begin.

---

1   Psalms 74:9

7: Faith in God

Faith, then, plays a key role in healing the world. But what *is* faith, and where does it come from?

If it appears that liberal Christianity tears faith down rather than building it up, that may be because you are mistaking faith for persuasion. Christianity may be the only religion in the world that makes a virtue out of unexamined belief. That is not faith.

We talked earlier about demons, and whether we must believe literally in demonology. We discussed alcoholism as a contemporary "demon" (a harmful power exceeding human strength), and how we should approach those held captive by this disease. This particular "demon" is interesting enough to examine closer. Remember: Jesus, empowered by the Spirit, went about doing good and healing those oppressed by such evils.

One thing recovering alcoholics tell us from experience is that the Spirit does indeed heal us. Alcoholics Anonymous members learned at its very beginning that success in beating their dependency required turning one's life over to a higher power. But *which* higher power? Surprisingly, they discovered that it does not seem to matter. What does matter is faith.[1]

---

1   From the Alcoholics Anonymous "Big Book": *We found that as soon as we were able to lay aside prejudice and express even a willingness to believe in a Power greater than ourselves, we commenced to get results, even though it was impossible for any of us to fully define or comprehend that Power, which is God. Much to our relief, we discovered we did not need to consider another's conception of God. Our own conception, however inadequate, was sufficient to make the approach and to affect a contact with Him. As soon as we admitted the possible existence of a Creative Intelligence, a Spirit of the Universe underlying the totality of things, we began to be possessed of a new sense of power and direction, provided we took other simple steps. ... As soon as a man can say that he does believe, or is willing to believe, we emphatically assure him that he is on his way. It has been repeatedly proven among us that upon this simple cornerstone a wonderfully effective spiritual structure can*

74   *Faith in God*

They also discovered another foundational Bible truth: that faith without works is dead. The steps of healing must be put into practice, and helping another is helping oneself. Through faith and through works, members of Alcoholics Anonymous are spreading the "good news"—their message of acceptance and healing—exactly what Jesus hoped for. Exactly what spiritual advisors in various religions today continue to hope for. God is with A.A. *Which* god, I do not know. I know only that this organization is a prime example of the power Jesus drew upon as he set a new humanitarian revolution in motion, based on godly compassion, understanding, and acceptance. The Kingdom is progressing.

Yet how is it possible to claim faith in God while knowing so little about him? Without knowing for sure that we even *have* a creator? I propose that this is where true faith enters the picture. For me, faith is trust that our existence has meaning, that we are uncovering its meaning, and that this meaning exists on a higher plane—call it the direction of a higher power if you wish—than simply going through the motions of life without purpose.

Faith is understood differently by different people. Let's look at the conclusions of a few other religious writers who have struggled to understand faith:

Marcus J. Borg: In modern English, this noun [faith] has acquired meanings that are quite different from its premodern meanings. ... Faith is often identified with believing [or as] a synonym for religion. "What faith are you?" means "What religion do you belong to?" But neither of these modern meanings is what faith meant in premodern Christianity. The ancient meanings are expressed by the Latin words *fidelitas* and *fiducia* and their Greek Equivalents. *Fidelitas* means "fidelity"—"faithfulness" ... commitment, loyalty, allegiance, and attentiveness to our relationship with God—in a Christian context, to God as known especially in Jesus. *Fiducia*

---

be built. This was great news to us, for we had assumed we could not make use of spiritual principles unless we accepted many things on faith which seemed difficult to believe. –Alcoholics Anonymous Fourth Edition, by A.A. World Services Inc, 2001, pp 46-47.

The River of Life 75

means "trust." ... It is also about deep trust in God. Here the opposite of faith is not infidelity, but "mistrust" —that is, anxiety. ...
Deep faith—as trust, *fiducia*—liberates us from anxiety. ... Think
of how differently faith as fidelity and trust is from faith as believing
a set of statements to be true. The latter can even increase anxiety.
For example, if we believe that there is a final judgment in which
we are sent to either heaven or hell, how could we not be anxious?[1]

Karen Armstrong: Faith is not about belief but about practice.
Religion is not about accepting twenty impossible propositions
before breakfast, but about doing the things that change you. ...
If you behave a certain way, you will be transformed. The myths
and laws of religion are not true because they conform to some
metaphysical, scientific, or historical reality but because they are
life enhancing. ... In the past, my own practice of religion had
diminished me, whereas true faith, I now believe, should make you
more human than before.[2]

The Dalai Lama: In the Buddhist tradition, we speak of three
different types of faith. The first is faith in the form of admiration
that you have toward a particular person or a particular state of
being. The second is aspiring faith. There is a sense of emulation;
you aspire to attain that state of being. The third type is the faith
of conviction. I feel that all three types of faith can be explained in
the Christian context as well. For example, a practicing Christian,
by reading the Gospel and reflecting on the life of Jesus, can have
a very strong devotion to and admiration for Jesus. That is the first
level of faith, the faith of admiration and devotion. After that, as
you strengthen your admiration and faith, it is possible to progress
to the second level, which is the faith of aspiration. In the Buddhist
tradition, you would aspire to buddhahood. In the Christian context you may not use the same language, but you can say that you
aspire to attain the full perfection of the divine nature, or union
with God. Then, once you have developed that sense of aspiration,

1   Marcus J. Borg, *Speaking Christian*, 2011, pp 120-122
2   Karen Armstrong, *The Spiral Staircase*, 2004, pp 270-271

you can develop a deep conviction that it is possible to perfect such a state of being. That is the third level of faith.[1]

John Dominic Crossan: Christian faith is always faith *in the historical Jesus as a manifestation of God to us.* ... Christian faith means finding in the picture of the historical Jesus the power and wisdom of God—and then getting serious about its implications for *our* lives, now. So faith goes beyond the historical facts to wrestle with their meanings. ... "Christ" is more than "Jesus," but not less. In short, if my faith in Christ doesn't interpret at the deepest level what I know about the historical Jesus, I'd better reexamine my faith.[2]

Susan Stover: *Clear faith* is a perspective, a way of seeing and being, that makes sense of the Bible as human-authored; views Jesus as an amazing human being; and views and trusts God as incomprehensible love. *Clear faith* is an unassuming, uncomplicated, and uncluttered trust in God that leads to a way of seeing, a way of life and being, centered in love. There are no required beliefs.[3]

I introduce myself as a Christian. I stand in awe of the life and teachings of Jesus, the man who lived 2,000 years ago. I want to be his disciple. I want to spread the message he taught. I have faith that this way of life works, that this way is godly and fulfilling, that this is our real purpose on earth. But I probably don't believe in the same god Jesus did, or the anthropomorphic god of various religions today. I am an agnostic, satisfied to leave God as a mystery, satisfied with the evidence of God-like workings in our lives without pretending to understand their cause. Is it possible to talk about God, to appreciate God, to even love God, while knowing to little about him?

---

1   The Dalai Lama, *The Good Heart,* 1996, pp 112-113
2   John Dominic Crossan & Richard G. Watts, *Who is Jesus?*, 1996, pp 139-140
3   Susan Stover, *Clear Faith*, 2011, p 40

The River of Life 77

The Bible tells us God is spirit.[1] Not *a spirit,* as the King James Version mistakenly translates, but simply spirit. We don't worship *a* spirit, we worship *in* spirit. God is not something we can point at, a person in a place, anymore than we can point at the Kingdom. God is Light, God is Life, God is Love. Of course, these claims all originate in those mysterious Johannine books (Revelation, John's Gospel, and the three Epistles of John), and this is admittedly a large part of the reason for my attraction to these books. I have learned in my search for God to look inward, not outward. These definitions of God highlight his immanence, not his transcendence. They give us experiential descriptions, explanations of the work of God that we can hang our hats on. We can say to one another, "that's a God thing," and nod knowingly in agreement. Where we feel love, we feel God. We share in awe, but we need not dissect the mystery of who or what God is in order to appreciate and enjoy godliness.

In the Fourth Gospel, Jesus claims these attributes in his own life. "I am the life." "I am the light." "I am the way." Either Jesus was directed by the Spirit of God, or he was himself God. You may choose whichever best fits your theology of incarnation; I see little practical difference between the two.

Yet I have met hundreds of people who trust in creeds, who lay out specific requirements that Christians must believe, requirements which leave me out in the cold, since I am quite poor at believing. "You must believe Jesus rose bodily from the dead." "You must believe Jesus died to save you from your sins." "You must believe God formed Adam six thousand years ago from the dust of the earth—we'll have none of that evolution nonsense!" But none of this has anything to do with my determination to follow Jesus' teachings, to learn from him as a disciple how to make this a better world. I do not attempt to merge my faith with my religious beliefs. I don't *have* any rigid religious beliefs to speak of.

Did Jesus believe in God? Yes, he did. Jesus held a vision of a better world, and in this vision, God is king. Jesus even named this utopia after God. He called it the Kingdom of God, envisioning a

---

1   John 4:24

world where God would return to earth and rule justly. Imagine a world governed by light, life, and love. As we've discussed already, this godly rule is on this earth, not up in heaven, and may or may not extend into the afterlife.

Will God someday set this world aside? Will we then float away to either heaven or hell? Perhaps, but these are mere *beliefs*. I do not personally believe these things, but if you do, I would not bother trying to change your mind, nor would I wish to. As my grandmother would say, "A man convinced against his will is of the same mind still." But this I believe:

And we know that all things work together for good to those who love God ...[1]

Do you believe this? Do you have faith? Because we are about to come full circle.

About two hundred years before Jesus, in the time of the Maccabees, belief in a resurrection began to make inroads into Judaism. When the Greek king Antiochus IV ruled, his persecution of the Jews grew so severe that it became hard to believe that the wrongs in life could be made right this side of the grave. The wrongs simply outweighed the rights. Justice, then, had to be found in an afterlife. But what would this afterlife be like?

While the books of the Maccabees may not exist in your Bible, they do in Catholic versions. A story is told in 2 Maccabees of a righteous woman and her seven sons who refused to eat unclean food, even when the king (Antiochus IV) tried to force them to eat swine. He tortured each one in turn, but they stayed true to God, and in their dying speeches they told us much about the coming resurrection. Who will be resurrected? *Those who obey the law of God.* What about those whose bodies are mutilated? *They will be resuscitated whole, with all of their limbs.* What will happen to the evil king? *He will die forever, never to live again.* But how can we believe in the power of resurrection? *By watching the birth of a new child, no less a miracle.*

---

1 Romans 8:28

The River of Life 79

By the time of Jesus, there was still much controversy about life after death. Many Jews, like the Sadducees, held no expectation of living again; the afterlife was an afterthought. But the Pharisees believed. They believed God would someday raise his people from their graves to walk again on earth among the living. They believed God would come down to earth and live with his people, like he did in the Garden of Eden. And they believed that in this age of God's rule, God would send forth his Spirit, just as Ezekiel promised.

Christians believed too, but their views were divided over the nature of this resurrection. Many held to the Jewish idea of a physical, bodily resurrection to live again on earth. Revelation espouses this view, and in time the resurrection of Jesus came to be understood this way.

But Paul saw things differently. Perhaps because of Hellenistic influence or perhaps because he saw the resurrected Jesus as a spiritual being in heaven, he had a different idea. He didn't believe in physical resuscitation, yet he recognized that Jesus' tomb was found empty. The body of Jesus had disappeared. Thus he imagined the resurrection of the dead would of necessity be "in body," though in a new, spiritual body, able to roam the heavens like Jesus. We would swap the old body for a new one.

John's Gospel presents a mystical third idea. It's not clear at all what its author believed about life after death, but we might guess that it would be similar to the way he describes Jesus' resurrection … in a manner that cannot be seen with human eyes, but which is very real and close to those still living.

So while the nature of life after death found little consensus, the first Christians did believe that the Kingdom would extend beyond this life. What we began would continue. I don't know if I believe in an afterlife—I reach out to the interconnectedness and sacredness of life, while finding it difficult to comprehend my own continued, *individual* existence after I die—but I have *faith*. I have faith that my life has purpose, it somehow matters, and continues to matter after I die.

I don't know what God is like beyond what I can experience through love, but the God I do know transcends and survives human death, and I have *faith in God.* Jesus showed this God to me, through his life and words. I concur with John's Gospel: Jesus *did* find the way to God. He found the way of life, the way of light, and it is only by following this path that we, too, can find God.

8: The River of Life

But when they came to Jesus and saw that he was already dead, they did not break his legs. But one of the soldiers pierced his side with a spear, and immediately blood and water came out.[1]

I believe a trickling river began that day, from the pierced side of Jesus. A river the prophets of Israel somehow anticipated.

There came out blood and water. Water, we are told by John's Gospel, represents the Spirit. The blood, while it carries many deep symbolic meanings, represents the sacrifice of Jesus, taking upon himself the covenantal punishment in our place, and ushering in the new *aion*. The age the prophets promised.

Six hundred years before Christ, a Jewish visionary named Ezekiel wrote down his depiction of a glorious new city under God's rule. Ezekiel wrote during a time of Jewish exile. Jerusalem had recently been conquered by the Babylonians, who razed Solomon's temple to the ground and deported the Jews into captivity. Ezekiel claims to have watched the glory of God depart from the temple.[2] God was punishing Israel, said Ezekiel, but soon his visions began to take on a different flavor. A flavor of redemption. After a period of suffering, God would one day reestablish Israel as God's favored people.

In Ezekiel's vision, God picked him up and carried him to a high mountain, where he could see what appeared to be a great walled city. This city had twelve gates, one for each of the twelve tribes of Israel. In the center of this city Ezekiel saw a new temple. Precise measurements depicted its height, breadth, and width. It contained rooms for preparing sacrifices; rooms for the priests; courtyards for worship. The dimensions of the altar were precisely

---

1   John 19:33-34
2   Ezekiel 10:1

82 *The River of Life*

specified, and the requirements for various offerings were made clear.

From the south side of the east gateway flowed a small river, ankle deep. Remember Isaiah's promise, telling of the day of the Lord's arrival? *For in the wilderness shall waters break out, and streams in the desert.* Zechariah, too, promised that in the Day of the Lord, living waters would flow out from Jerusalem, both to the west into the Mediterranean Sea and to the east into the Dead Sea.[1] As Ezekiel watched the river flow, it deepened until it became knee deep, then too deep for one to wade across. Trees grew on each side of the river; fruit trees of all kinds, which bore fruit every month of the year, and the leaves of which never turned brown. This fruit, Ezekiel saw, served both as food and as healing balm.

Everywhere this river flowed, life bloomed. When the river reached the Dead Sea, the salt water there turned fresh, and the sea began to teem with new life.

Six and a half centuries later, in the latter half of the first century, some 50 years or so after Christ died, another man saw the same city.[2] Like Ezekiel, John of Patmos was carried in the spirit to a high maintain, where he saw the same vision. John describes this city—the "New Jerusalem"—in even grander terms than Ezekiel. The foundation is of precious stones, the buildings are pure gold, and the gates are made of pearls. The mysterious city of Ezekiel, we now learn from John of Patmos, floats down from heaven to replace the recently destroyed Jerusalem of John's day. The walls are stronger, over 200 feet thick. Never would Jerusalem be destroyed again.

However, one important item is missing from the city the way John sees it:

But I saw no temple in it ...

---

1   Zechariah 14:8

2   This dating of the book of Revelation to around the year 80 CE derives from my research as presented in the book *Revelation: The Way It Happened.* Admittedly, my opinion differs from the majority in this matter.

The River of Life 83

What happened to the temple? Ezekiel was very clear about its existence, complete with measurements and sacrificial instructions. Where did it go?

The answer lies in the rest of the verse:

... for the Lord God Almighty and the Lamb are its temple. [1]

Ezekiel's temple has been replaced by Jesus, the final sacrifice. John's Gospel is even more explicit about this transformation:

Jesus answered and said to them, "Destroy this temple, and in three days I will raise it up." Then the Jews said, "It has taken forty-six years to build this temple, and will you raise it up in three days?" But he was speaking of the temple of his body. [2]

A number of Christians today still anticipate the rebuilding of the Jewish temple, but I believe they misunderstand how thoroughly Jesus replaced the temple age according to the Bible. A new *aion* has arrived, with its own temple. A temple for all the world, which will recognize no abominations. Johannine literature could hardly be clearer on the topic: the new temple has already been built. It was built three days after Jesus died.

What does this mean for the river of life that Ezekiel saw flowing out from the temple? John's vision in the book of Revelation continues:

And he showed me a pure river of water of life, clear as crystal, proceeding from the throne of God and of the Lamb. In the middle of its street, and on either side of the river, was the tree of life, which bore twelve fruits, each tree yielding its fruit every month. The leaves of the tree were for the healing of the nations. [3]

The river of life. Isaiah's river, Zechariah's river, Ezekiel's river. It's still there, flowing out from the new temple: the resurrected Jesus. Past the old Jerusalem flows this river. Past the fallen temple of a bygone era. The covenantal punishments are over, and the time

---

1   Revelation 21:20
2   John 2:19-21
3   Revelation 22:1-2

84   *The River of Life*

of healing has begun. God's age has arrived. And as the river flows, it grows wider, deeper, as others join in:

But whoever drinks of the water that I shall give him will never thirst. But the water that I shall give him will become in him a fountain of water springing up into everlasting life.[1]

He who believes in me, as the Scripture has said, out of his heart will flow rivers of living water.[2]

This living water continues to flow out from Jesus today, growing deeper and grander as it gathers followers, bringing life to everything it touches in the world. The prophets were right: today there are over two billion Christians worldwide, and many others who have discovered the same truths. Should we not be able to make a difference?

Participatory eschatology. This is my religion. This is Jesus' dream, and it is happening. This world will become what we, through the help of God and the inspiration and example of Jesus our Savior, transform it into.

---

1   John 4:14

2   John 7:38

Also from Energion Publications

... thought-provoking from cover to cover.

The Dubious Disciple

Also by Lee Harmon

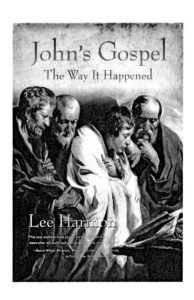

MORE FROM ENERGION PUBLICATIONS

Personal Study
Holy Smoke! Unholy Fire	Bob McKibben	$14.99
The Jesus Paradigm	David Alan Black	$17.99
When People Speak for God	Henry Neufeld	$17.99
The Sacred Journey	Chris Surber	$11.99

Christian Living
It's All Greek to Me	David Alan Black	$3.99
Grief: Finding the Candle of Light	Jody Neufeld	$8.99
My Life Story	Becky Lynn Black	$14.99
Crossing the Street	Robert LaRochelle	$16.99
Life as Pilgrimage	David Moffett-Moore	14.99

Bible Study
Learning and Living Scripture	Lentz/Neufeld	$12.99
From Inspiration to Understanding	Edward W. H. Vick	$24.99
Philippians: A Participatory Study Guide	Bruce Epperly	$9.99
Ephesians: A Participatory Study Guide	Robert D. Cornwall	$9.99
Ecclesiastes: A Participatory Study Guide	Russell Meek	$9.99

Theology
Creation in Scripture	Herold Weiss	$12.99
Creation: the Christian Doctrine	Edward W. H. Vick	$12.99
The Politics of Witness	Allan R. Bevere	$9.99
Ultimate Allegiance	Robert D. Cornwall	$9.99
History and Christian Faith	Edward W. H. Vick	$9.99
The Journey to the Undiscovered Country	William Powell Tuck	$9.99
Process Theology	Bruce G. Epperly	$4.99

Ministry
Clergy Table Talk	Kent Ira Groff	$9.99
Out of This World	Darren McClellan	$24.99

Generous Quantity Discounts Available
Dealer Inquiries Welcome
Energion Publications — P.O. Box 841
Gonzalez, FL_ 32560
Website: http://energionpubs.com
Phone: (850) 525-3916